REVISE PEARSON EDEXC GCSE (9–1)
Business

PRACTICE PAPERS Plus+

Series Consultant: Harry Smith
Authors: Paul Clark and Andrew Redfern

These Practice Papers are designed to complement your revision and to help prepare you for the exams. They do not include all the content and skills needed for the complete course and have been written to help you practise what you have learned. They may not be representative of a real exam paper. Remember that the official Pearson specification and associated assessment guidance materials are the only authoritative source of information and should always be referred to for definitive guidance.

For further information, go to **quals.pearson.com**

Question difficulty
Look at this scale next to each exam-style question. It tells you how difficult the question is.

Contents

		Question Paper	Answers
SET 1	Paper 1	1	125
	Paper 2	21	129
SET 2	Paper 1	42	133
	Paper 2	62	137
SET 3	Paper 1	83	141
	Paper 2	103	145

About this book

The practice papers in this book are designed to help you prepare for your Pearson Edexcel GCSE Business examinations.

In the margin of each paper you will find:
- links to relevant pages in the Revise Pearson Edexcel GCSE Business (9–1) Revision Guide
- hints to get you started on tricky questions, or to help you avoid common pitfalls
- help or reminders about important phrases or key terms
- advice on how to get top marks in the higher-level questions.

If you want to tackle a paper under exam conditions, you could cover up the hints in the margin.

There are also answers to all the questions at the back of the book, together with information about how marks are allocated. Many of these are sample model student answers, especially for the longer writing questions. This means that there are many answers which could be given, so you could answer the question differently and still gain full marks. The model answer could still give you new ideas to help you to improve an answer.

About the papers

Look at the time guidance at the top of each paper if you wish to practise under exam conditions. Remember that in the exam:
- You should use a black ink or ball-point pen.
- You should read every question carefully and answer all the questions in the space provided.
- Try to check your answers if you have time at the end.

Good luck!

Set 1
Paper 1

SECTION A
Answer ALL questions.
Write your answers in the spaces provided.
Some questions must be answered with a cross in a box ☒.
If you change your mind about an answer, put a line through the box ☒
and then mark your new answer with a cross ☒.

Revision Guide
Page 17

1 (a) Which **one** of the following is an example of a variable cost?
     Select **one** answer.   (1)

   ☐ **A** Rent
   ☐ **B** Wages
   ☐ **C** Loan repayments
   ☐ **D** Buildings insurance

LEARN IT!

Variable costs vary depending on the number of products produced or the amount of work done.

(b) Which **one** of the following is an example of a customer need?
     Select **one** answer.   (1)

   ☐ **A** Differentiation
   ☐ **B** Profit
   ☐ **C** Convenience
   ☐ **D** Customer feedback

Revision Guide
Pages 6–7

Hint

First, rule out the options you know are incorrect.

(c) Explain **one** reason why a business would carry out market research.   (3)

....
....
....
....
....
....
....

Revision Guide
Page 8

LEARN IT!

Market research is the process of gathering information about the market and customers' needs and wants. It will help inform business decisions, including product design and marketing, identify gaps in the market and reduce risk.

Set 1 Paper 1

Revision Guide Page 6

Hint
When answering 3-mark 'Explain' questions state one benefit and then develop your answer by explaining two linked points, using connectives such as 'because' and 'therefore'.

(d) Explain **one** benefit to a business of increasing its range of products. (3)

....
....
....
....
....
....
....
....

(Total for Question 1 = 8 marks)

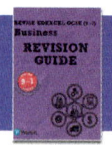

Revision Guide Pages 31–32

LEARN IT!
A business plan identifies the business idea, its aims and objectives, the target market, forecasts of revenue, cost, profit and cash-flow, sources of finance, the business's location and its marketing mix. Business plans help minimise risk and are needed to obtain finance.

2 (a) Which **two** of the following are features of a business plan? Select **two** answers. (2)

☐ A Job description
☐ B Social media posts
☐ C Cash-flow forecast
☐ D Business aims and objectives
☐ E Employment legislation

Revision Guide Page 3

Watch out!
Some multiple-choice questions will ask for you to identify **two** correct responses.

(b) Which **two** of the following describe the purpose of business activity? Select **two** answers. (2)

☐ A To take risks
☐ B To meet customer needs
☐ C To carry out market research
☐ D To produce goods and services
☐ E To make decisions about how resources are used

2

Figure 1 contains information about a small business for one month's trading.

The business has estimated that it needs to sell 180 units per month in order to break even.

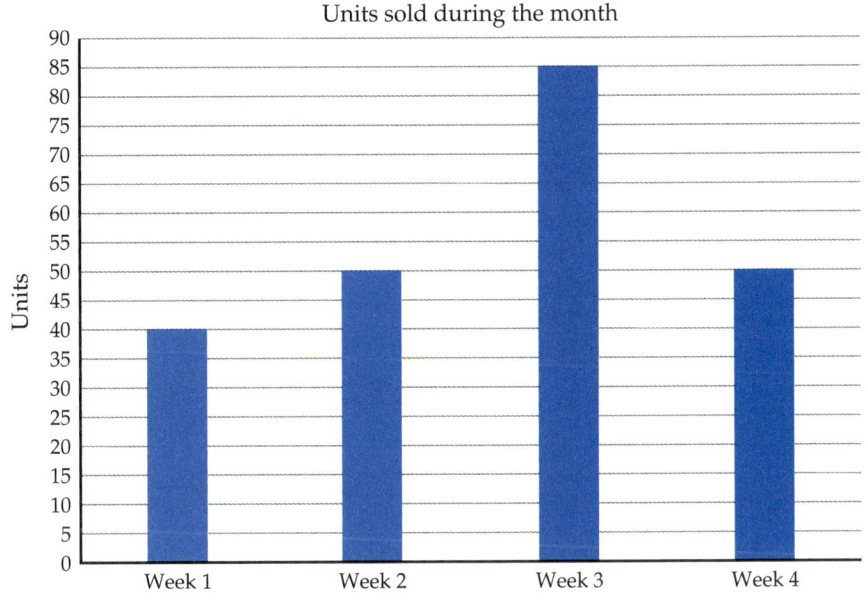

Figure 1

(c) Using the information in Figure 1, calculate the margin of safety for the business. You are advised to show your workings. (2)

.... units

Revision Guide
Page 20

Hint

You have been given the break-even point. You now need to work out total sales for the month.

Hint

To calculate the margin of safety subtract the break-even sales from the actual or budgeted sales.

Maths skills You may be given a calculation mark, even if the final answer you give is incorrect, so make sure you show all your workings as clearly as possible. A mark may still be awarded if you have made a mistake in your calculation but used the correct approach/formula.

Set 1 Paper 1

Revision Guide
Page 12

LEARN IT!

A market map can be used to position and compare products in a market, and to identify opportunities in the market where customer needs are not being met.

Hint

A business owner might use a market map when carrying out market research – in particular, when analysing competition.

Revision Guide
Page 40

LEARN IT!

An interest rate is the percentage payment over a period of time that is given to savers on savings or paid by borrowers on loans.

Hint

Explain how a rise in interest rates affects businesses through rising costs, or how businesses are affected by a fall in demand due to the higher cost of borrowing for consumers.

(d) Explain **one** reason that a business owner might use a market map. (3)

....
....
....
....
....
....
....
....

(e) Explain **one** disadvantage to a business of an increase in interest rates. (3)

....
....
....
....
....
....
....
....

(Total for Question 2 = 12 marks)

3 (a) Which **one** of the following is a feature of a franchise?
Select **one** answer. (1)

- [ ] A The franchisee keeps all profits
- [ ] B The business has unlimited liability
- [ ] C The franchisee can sell shares in the business
- [ ] D The business has limited liability

Table 1 gives the cash-flow forecast for a small business.

	Jan (£)	Feb (£)	Mar (£)
Cash inflow	8 500	20 200	8 200
Cash outflow	5 500	....	5 500
Net cash-flow	3 000	12 900	2 700
Opening balance	−2 000	1 000	13 900
Closing balance	....	13 900	16 600

Table 1

(b) Complete Table 1 by calculating the missing values.
You are advised to show your workings. (2)

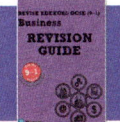

Set 1 Paper 1

Revision Guide Pages 29–30

Hint

You could refer to any one of the 4 Ps of the marketing mix (product, price, promotion or place).

Revision Guide Pages 13–14

LEARN IT!

A market is competitive when there are a large number of businesses relative to the number of potential customers. Competition is high in markets where businesses sell very similar products and services that are difficult to differentiate.

Hint

When answering 3-mark 'Explain' questions you need to make a **point** (a reason, advantage or drawback) then provide **two linked strands of development** using connective statements such as 'this leads to' and 'as a result'.

(c) Explain **one** way a business can use the marketing mix to improve competitiveness. (3)

....
....
....
....
....
....
....
....

(d) Explain **one** disadvantage of setting up a business in a location close to its competitors. (3)

....
....
....
....
....
....
....
....

(e) Discuss how stakeholders can affect business decisions. (6)

....
....
....
....
....
....
....
....
....
....
....
....
....
....
....
....
....

(Total for Question 3 = 15 marks)

TOTAL FOR SECTION A = 35 MARKS

Set 1 Paper 1

Revision Guide
Pages 33–34

Hint

Give specific examples of how the stakeholder can affect business decisions. Consider what different stakeholders want and potential conflicts of interest.

LEARN IT!

A stakeholder is an individual or a group that has an interest in and is affected by the activities of a business. Stakeholders might include owners (shareholders), managers, employees, customers, suppliers, government, the local community and pressure groups.

Approaching the question

You could answer this question in one of two ways:

- You could make two separate points (two stakeholder groups) in two clear paragraphs, which together contain a total of five linked strands of development.

- You could provide one point (one stakeholder group) in one paragraph, with a total of five linked strands of development arising from the point you make.

7

SECTION B

Answer ALL questions.

Read the following extract carefully and then answer Questions 4, 5 and 6.

Write your answers in the spaces provided.

Sid is the owner of *Bluecoat Builders Ltd*, a small building company that specialises in loft conversions. Sid started the company 12 years ago and now employs four full-time builders. In that time, *Bluecoat Builders* has developed a reputation for excellent customer service. Most of Sid's new customers now come through recommendations from customers' friends and family.

Bluecoat Builders' trade is seasonal, with the majority of work coming in the summer months when it is more convenient to carry out work on roofs. To boost sales in the winter months, Sid has introduced a special offer of free decoration (paint or wallpaper) with all loft conversions from December to February.

For each job, Sid has to hire scaffolding from a local company, which can be very expensive. In the long-term, Sid has decided it would be cheaper to buy the scaffolding so that the company owns it as an asset. The scaffolding will cost £3 500.

As a building company, *Bluecoat Builders* has to comply with UK Building Regulations 2010. For example, every loft conversion the company completes must receive an energy performance certificate following an inspection by the local council.

Set 1 Paper 1

Revision Guide Pages 3, 4 and 7

4 (a) Outline **one** benefit to *Bluecoat Builders* of having a reputation for excellent customer service. (2)

....
....
....

Hint

Customer service is one way that a business can add value. Be careful to say how this will benefit Sid (not his customers).

(b) Analyse the impact on *Bluecoat Builders* of UK building regulations legislation. (6)

....
....
....
....
....
....
....
....
....
....
....
....
....
....
....

Watch out!

For 2-mark 'Outline' questions, give a benefit, a linked expansion point and refer to context to gain both marks.

Revision Guide Page 36

Watch out!

In this question, you are being asked to 'Analyse the impact', so you can discuss the benefits, the drawbacks or a combination of both. If you are taking a two-paragraph approach, then you can discuss either two benefits of the legislation on *Bluecoat Builders*, or two drawbacks, or one benefit and one drawback.

(Total for Question 4 = 8 marks)

Approaching the question

In this question you are marked in two skills areas.

- **Analysis**: You need to include one or two valid points and at least five linked strands of development. Remember to use connectives such as 'therefore', 'this leads to' and 'because' to show this.
- **Application**: To obtain marks for Application, you should refer to the context throughout – so your answer needs to be relevant to *Bluecoat Builders* and UK building regulations.

Set 1 Paper 1

5 One impact of legislation on businesses is that it results in additional costs being incurred.
Sid has drawn up the following financial information.

Annual fixed costs	£150 000
Average cost per loft conversion	£11 000
Average price customers pay for a loft conversion	£38 000

Table 1

Revision Guide Page 19

Hint

Break-even is the level of output at which a business's revenue covers its total costs.

You can work out the **break-even point in units** by using the formula:

$$\frac{\text{Fixed cost}}{\text{Sales price} - \text{Variable cost}}$$

If you multiply this by the sales price you get the break-even point in revenue.

Maths skills Start by writing out the formula for break-even before substituting in the relevant figures from Table 1.

(a) Using the information in Table 1, calculate to the nearest whole number, the number of loft conversions *Bluecoat Builders* would need to install each year in order to break even. You are advised to show your workings. (2)

.... units

Sid has learned that the cost for the council building inspector to review the work of all local builders is to increase by 17 per cent. On *Bluecoat Builders'* last project, the building inspection cost £250.

Revision Guide Page 88

Hint

You have been given two pieces of information (a percentage increase of 17 per cent and the cost of the original building inspection). Use this to work out how much more *Bluecoat Builders* will need to pay.

(b) Calculate, to two decimal places, how much more *Bluecoat Builders* will have to pay for its work to be inspected after the increase in cost. You are advised to show your workings. (2)

£ ....

(c) Analyse the impact on *Bluecoat Builders* of its business being seasonal. (6)

....
....
....
....
....
....
....
....
....
....
....
....
....
....
....

(Total for Question 5 = 10 marks)

Set 1 Paper 1

Revision Guide Page 22

Hint

Consider how Sid's cash-flow will be affected at different times of the year. What might be the consequence of having a negative cash-flow in the winter months?

Watch out!

This question is asking you to 'Analyse the impact', so you will need to discuss the benefits, the drawbacks or a combination of both, as impacts can be positive or negative. If you are taking a two-paragraph approach (analysing two points) then you can discuss either two benefits for *Bluecoat Builders*, or two drawbacks, or one benefit and one drawback.

Approaching the question

To demonstrate **Analysis** for this question, you need to give **one or two clear points** and a minimum of **five linked strands of development**. Use connectives such as 'this means that', 'as a result' and 'therefore' to show the links you make.

Remember to demonstrate **Application** by making your answer specific to *Bluecoat Builders*. You can use words and phrases from the case study, such as 'small building company', 'four full-time builders' and 'free decoration (paint or wallpaper) with all loft conversions'.

Set 1 Paper 1

Revision Guide Pages 15–16

Hint

Business objectives may be financial (profit, market share, financial security) or non-financial (independence and control, customer satisfaction, recognition, personal satisfaction).

Watch out!

'State' questions test **Application**, so you must include context, using words and phrases associated with *Bluecoat Builders* that do not appear in the question, such as 'loft conversions' and 'building work'.

Revision Guide Page 26

Hint

Think about the key differences between a sole trader and a limited company. How might these affect aspects of running a business such as liability, the ability to raise finance and being able to take time off?

6 (a) State **one** objective Sid might set for his business. (1)

....

....

....

(b) Outline **one** benefit to Sid of running a private limited company. (2)

....

....

....

....

....

....

Sid is considering two options for raising £3 500 to purchase the scaffolding, so that the company owns it as an asset.

Option 1: Taking out a bank loan.

Option 2: Using retained profit.

(c) Justify which **one** of these two options *Bluecoat Builders* should choose. (9)

....
....
....
....
....
....
....
....
....
....
....
....
....
....
....
....
....
....
....
....

(Total for Question 6 = 12 marks)

TOTAL FOR SECTION B = 30 MARKS

Set 1 Paper 1

Approaching the question

In the 9-mark 'Justify' questions, you will always be given two options to choose from. There is no need to discuss both options. You can gain maximum marks by referring to one option only.

Therefore, the simplest structure for answering this question is to focus on one option and adopt a three-paragraph approach:

- Paragraph 1: Make a judgement about which option you feel is best. There is not one 'right' option – you could choose either. Explain why you have chosen this option. Aim to include at least three linked strands of development, so that you demonstrate **Analysis**.

- Paragraph 2: State the drawback of the option you have chosen; this will help you show balance and count towards **Evaluation**. Aim to include at least three further linked strands of development.

By including three linked strands of development in each paragraph, you will be more confident that you are covering the overall requirement of five linked strands of development for this answer.

- Paragraph 3: Conclude your response by stating the main reason for your decision; in this case, why *Bluecoat Builders* should choose a bank loan/retained profit. Try to include a sophisticated 'evaluative technique' in your conclusion, such as using the 'It depends' rule.

The 'It depends' rule is an important way to help you score highly for **Evaluation**. Once you have stated your conclusion, consider additional factors that might influence the decision, introducing these with 'It depends' and explaining what the effect might be.

Ensure you refer to the context throughout to demonstrate **Application**. This means including language specifically related to the context of building loft conversions.

SECTION C

Answer ALL questions.

Read the following extract carefully and then answer Question 7.

Write your answers in the spaces provided.

Spectrum Paints was established by Dafne Forbes in 2012. The company manufactures a unique range of paints for domestic customers. *Spectrum Paints* is a premium brand distributed through small independent home improvement retailers. As such, it is not a large company and its products are not as well known as other paint brands such as *Crown* or *Dulux*. Neither is its product offering stocked in major retailers such as *B&Q*.

The company's unique selling point is its 'Trio Range', a pack of three paints in a set of complementary colours to decorate a room.

As the company has grown, its current manufacturing facilities are no longer suitable and Dafne is looking for larger premises. Dafne would like the new premises to be big enough to include a showroom and shop, so that customers can buy direct from *Spectrum Paints*.

Spectrum Paints imports most of the materials that are used to make its emulsion paints. Many of the raw materials are manufactured using crude oil and so they are affected by global oil prices. Over the past three years oil prices have been rising and this has increased the company's costs. Dafne has explored a number of options to help boost revenue in light of these external influences.

Set 1 Paper 1

Revision Guide Page 28

Hint
Consider proximity to a range of factors, such as customers, competition and transport links.

Watch out!
'State' questions test **Application**, so you must include words such as 'decorating shop' that do not appear in the question.

Revision Guide Page 75

Hint
Start by fully understanding what each axis represents and what the graph is actually plotting.

Revision Guide Page 38

Hint
If someone is earning less money, they have less disposable income to spend on home improvements.

7 (a) State **one** factor Dafne might consider when choosing a new location for *Spectrum Paints*. (1)

....
....
....

Figure 2 shows the price of Brent crude oil per barrel between 2014 and 2018.

Figure 2

(b) Identify the years when Brent crude oil prices fell below $40 per barrel. (1)

....
....

(c) Outline **one** way that a fall in consumer incomes could affect *Spectrum Paints*. (2)

....
....
....
....
....

Dafne has identified two ways that could help *Spectrum Paints* increase its revenue.

Option 1: Launch a new range of paint.

Option 2: Increase its current prices by 5 per cent.

(d) Justify which **one** of these two options Dafne should choose. (9)

....

....

....

....

....

....

....

....

....

....

....

....

....

....

....

....

....

....

....

....

....

....

....

....

....

Set 1 Paper 1

Revision Guide Page 29

Hint

This question is about the marketing mix. How can a business be more competitive through developing its products and changing their prices?

LEARN IT!

Businesses use the marketing mix (the 4 Ps of product, place, promotion and price) in order to provide products and services that meet customers' needs while generating a profit for the business.

Watch out!

Increasing price will increase the contribution per pot of paint, but it could also lower demand if customers are not willing to pay the higher price.

Hint

See page 18 for guidance on how to approach this question.

Set 1 Paper 1

Approaching the question

In the 9-mark 'Justify' questions, you will always be given two options to choose from. There is no need to discuss both options. You can gain maximum marks by referring to one option only.

Therefore, the simplest structure for answering this question is to focus on one option and adopt a three-paragraph approach.

- Paragraph 1: Make a judgement about which option you feel is best – you can choose either. Explain why you think this is. Aim to include at least three linked strands of development, so that you demonstrate **Analysis**.

- Paragraph 2: State the drawback of the option you have chosen; this will help you show balance and count towards **Evaluation**. Aim to include at least three further linked strands of development.

By including three linked strands of development in both paragraphs, you will be more confident that you are covering the overall requirement of five linked strands of development for this answer.

- Paragraph 3: Conclude your response by stating the main reason for your decision; in this case, why *Spectrum Paints* should choose to launch a new range of paints/increase prices by 5 per cent. Try to include a sophisticated 'evaluative technique' in your conclusion, such as using the 'It depends' rule to demonstrate factors that could change your decision.

Ensure you refer to the context throughout to demonstrate **Application**. This means including language specifically related to the context of paint.

The value of the pound has increased in recent months.

(e) Evaluate whether the value of the pound will help *Spectrum Paints* become more competitive in its market. You should use the information provided as well as your knowledge of business. (12)

Set 1 Paper 1

Revision Guide Page 41

Hint

You could start your answer by analysing how a stronger pound could help *Spectrum Paints* reduce its costs. Think about how exchange rates affect importers and exporters. Remember that exchange rates are constantly fluctuating, and the value of the pound could also fall.

LEARN IT!

The exchange rate is the price of buying foreign currency. It tells people and businesses how much foreign currency they get for every pound.

Watch out!

To demonstrate the skill of **Analysis** throughout your answer, make sure you do the following.

- Ensure your answer has a minimum of **five linked strands of development**. These can be spread across the two points you make.
- Use connectives, such as 'this means that', 'therefore' and 'this leads to', to demonstrate the links you make.

Set 1 Paper 1

Watch out!

To show the skill of **Application** throughout your answer, make sure you do the following.

- Refer to the home decoration market and to *Spectrum Paints* itself, as well as to *Spectrum Paint's* competitors, *Dulux* and *Crown*.
- Use phrases from the case study such as 'unique range of paints', 'small independent home improvement retailers', 'showroom and shop', 'emulsion paints' and 'crude oil'.

Hint

In your conclusion it is useful to apply the 'It depends' rule, as the answer to an 'Evaluate' question may depend on a factor not mentioned. For example, the extent that the exchange rate will help *Spectrum Paints* become more competitive may depend on how much the value of the pound has risen against other key currencies.

....
....
....
....
....
....
....

(Total for Question 7 = 25 marks)

TOTAL FOR SECTION C = 25 MARKS

TOTAL FOR PAPER = 90 MARKS

Approaching the question

'Evaluate' questions test all four skill areas.

Understanding: Give clear definitions and use business terminology throughout your answer.

Application: Refer to *Spectrum Paints* throughout your response. A good way of doing this is by using specific words and phrases from the case study, such as 'pack of three paints' or 'showroom and shop'.

Analysis: Include a minimum of five linked strands of development; they can be spread across the two points you make. Show your links using connectives such as 'this means that…', 'therefore…' and 'this leads to…'

Evaluation: Present a balanced argument. You must argue why the value of the pound will help *Spectrum Paints*, but you must also suggest why it may not / why other economic factors (for example, consumer incomes, interest rates or unemployment levels) may also play a significant role. Finally, give a balanced conclusion, making use of the 'It depends' argument.

SECTION A

Answer ALL questions.
Write your answers in the spaces provided.
Some questions must be answered with a cross in a box ☒.
If you change your mind about an answer, put a line through the box ☒
and then mark your new answer with a cross ☒.

1 (a) Which **one** of the following is a non-financial method of motivation?
Select **one** answer. (1)

☐ A Bonus
☐ B Autonomy
☐ C Remuneration
☐ D Commission

(b) Which **one** of the following is **not** an element of the marketing mix?
Select **one** answer. (1)

☐ A Production
☐ B Product
☐ C Promotion
☐ D Place

(c) Explain **one** benefit to a business of training its employees. (3)

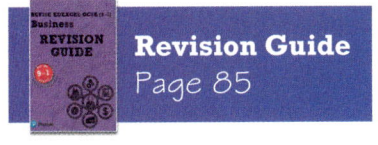

....
....
....
....
....
....
....

Set 1 Paper 2

Revision Guide Page 85

LEARN IT!
Remember, non-financial methods of motivation are ways of encouraging employees to work well that do not involve giving them money directly.

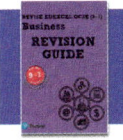

Revision Guide Page 66

Hint
Immediately aim to rule out the options you know are incorrect.

Revision Guide Page 83

Hint
When answering a 3-mark 'Explain' question, make sure you state one benefit then develop your answer by explaining two linked points, using connectives such as 'because' and 'therefore'.

21

Set 1 Paper 2

Revision Guide Page 50

LEARN IT!

Stock market flotation is when a business issues shares for sale on the stock exchange.

(d) Explain **one** reason why a business may undertake a stock market flotation. (3)

....
....
....
....
....
....

(Total for Question 1 = 8 marks)

Revision Guide Page 80

Hint

Other roles within business include directors, senior managers, operational staff and support staff.

2 (a) Which **two** of the following are examples of key responsibilities of team leaders?
Select **two** answers. (2)

☐ A Business target-setting and strategy formation
☐ B Providing services that support the main function of a business
☐ C Overall business performance
☐ D Performance management of some workers
☐ E Providing training, support and motivation

Revision Guide Page 73

LEARN IT!

You can find **gross profit** by calculating:

Sales revenue − Cost of sales

Gross profit is the profit made from a business's trading activities before other operating costs and interest have been deducted.

(b) Which **two** of the following are most likely to increase a business's gross profit?
Select **two** answers. (2)

☐ A An increase in product sales
☐ B A reduction in the interest paid by the business on its loans
☐ C Other operating expenses fall by 10 per cent
☐ D A reduction in the cost of sales
☐ E Paying less rent for the business premises

Figure 1 shows a bar gate stock graph of two deliveries for a business, marked A and B.

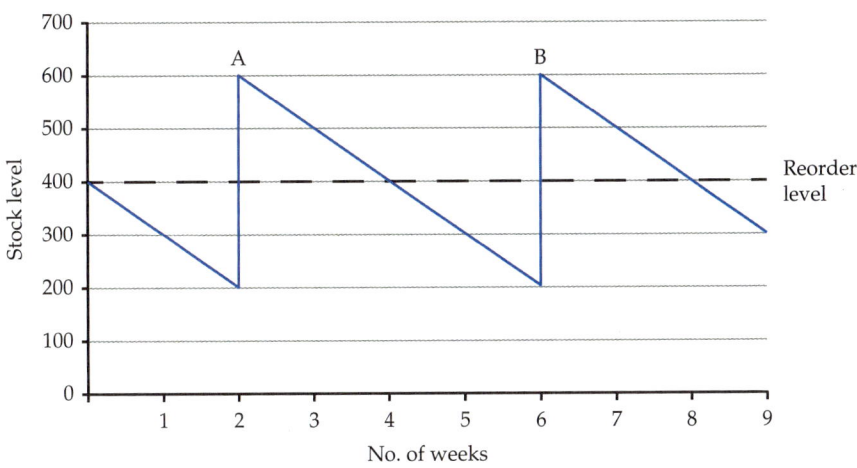

Figure 1

 (c) Using the information in Figure 1, calculate the lead time of delivery B. You are advised to show your workings. (2)

.... weeks

Revision Guide Page 69

LEARN IT!

The lead time is the time taken between ordering supplies and those supplies being delivered.

Maths skills You may gain a calculation mark even if your final answer is incorrect, so make sure you show all your workings as clearly as possible.

Set 1 Paper 2

Revision Guide
Page 57

Hint

If a question asks you to 'Explain **one** impact...' then you can explain either a positive or a negative impact. Make sure you write **two linked strands of development** to explain how your chosen impact affects a business.

Revision Guide
Page 71

LEARN IT!

Make sure you know the difference between quality assurance and quality control. In a quality assurance system, every member of staff is responsible for the quality of their work throughout the production process. In a quality control system, standards are checked at the end of the production line.

(d) Explain **one** impact that pressure group activity may have on a business. (3)

....

....

....

....

....

....

....

....

(e) Explain **one** benefit to a business of implementing a quality assurance system. (3)

....

....

....

....

....

....

....

....

(Total for Question 2 = 12 marks)

3 (a) Which **one** of the following is an advantage of being a public limited company?
Select **one** answer. (1)

☐ **A** The company can issue share capital

☐ **B** It is now less likely that the company can be taken over

☐ **C** The company's financial performance will be kept private

☐ **D** The company will have unlimited liability

Figure 2 shows the price level of a product (Product A) for a business over three years.

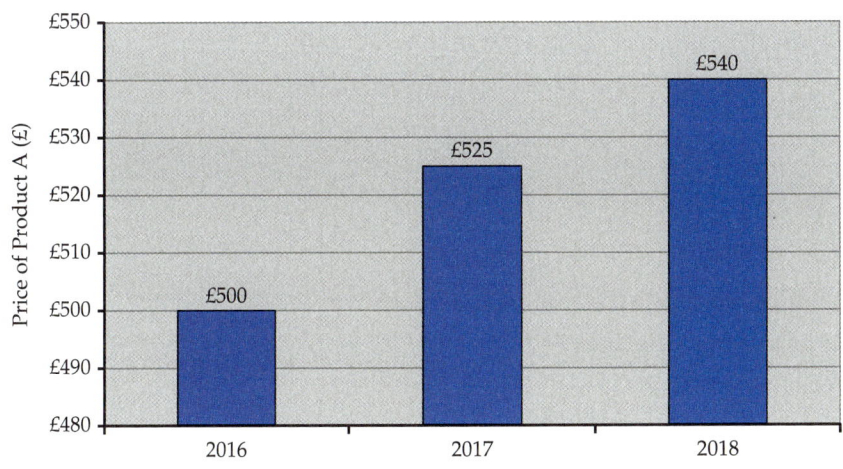

Figure 2

(b) Using the information in Figure 2, calculate the percentage increase in price between 2016 and 2018. You are advised to show your workings. (2)

.... %

Revision Guide
Page 50

Hint

A private limited company (Ltd) can change its status to become a public limited company (PLC) through a stock market flotation.

Revision Guide
Page 88

Maths skills When calculating percentage change, you need to work out the difference between the two numbers then divide this figure by the original number and multiply by 100.

Maths skills You may gain a calculation mark, even if your final answer is incorrect, so make sure you show all your working out as clearly as possible.

Set 1 Paper 2

Revision Guide
Page 76

Hint

Think about a specific piece of financial data that a business may be able to use – for example, sales/revenue figures, costs, financial accounts, interest rates, tax rates. Then develop your answer by explaining two linked points, using connectives such as 'this means that' and 'because'.

Revision Guide
Page 81

LEARN IT!

Recruiting externally is when a business appoints a new employee from outside of the organisation rather than selecting someone who already works for the business.

Hint

For this question, you need to ensure your answer focuses on the critical word 'externally'.

(c) Explain **one** way a business might use financial data to help make a decision. (3)

....
....
....
....
....
....
....
....

(d) Explain **one** drawback to a business of recruiting employees externally. (3)

....
....
....
....
....
....
....
....

(e) Discuss the benefit to a business of having a differentiated product. (6)

....
....
....
....
....
....
....
....
....
....
....
....

(Total for Question 3 = 15 marks)

TOTAL FOR SECTION A = 35 MARKS

Set 1 Paper 2

Revision Guide Page 60

Watch out!

Time is limited in the exam – there is roughly 1 minute for every mark – so you cannot afford to waste time. One way you can do this is by making sure you don't start your response by repeating the question; for example, for this question, don't start by saying, 'One benefit to a business of having a highly differentiated product is ...' While this approach won't lose you marks, it will take up valuable time.

Approaching the question

As this question starts with, 'Discuss the benefit', you must only talk about the positives of having a differentiated product. You can do this by providing **one** benefit with **five linked strands of development**, or by providing **two** benefits with **five linked strands of development** across the two points. You may find it easier to answer 6-mark 'Discuss' questions using two separate points, since to try to develop five linked strands around one point could cause you to drift away from the focus of the question.

SECTION B

Answer ALL questions.
Read the following extract carefully and then answer Questions 4, 5 and 6.
Write your answers in the spaces provided.

Subway® is the world's largest submarine sandwich chain with more than 42 500 locations around the world, and over 2 500 locations in the United Kingdom. Subway has become the leading choice for people seeking quick personalised meals that the whole family can enjoy. In creating the sandwiches, Subway produces sandwiches made to order (job production); the customer can choose the type of bread and salad items that go into their 'Sub'.

Recently, Subway has reviewed its Corporate Social Responsibility (ethical) policies in a number of areas and has made a commitment to be a socially responsible business. For instance, it has stated its commitment in helping to tackle childhood obesity, by taking on the challenge to reduce sugar found in Subway products and in the ingredients provided by third party suppliers. It has also recently been the proud recipient of an award from Compassion in Farming for its commitment to using only free range eggs in all Subway products across Europe.

Demand for Subway products is growing and to ensure that the needs of customers are met, Subway has recently trialled delivery through Just Eat. The world-famous 'Subs' can now be ordered through both the Just Eat app and website, from 1 030 stores across the UK including over 450 stores in London, Leeds and Manchester*. 'Sub' fans can order at any time of the day, including weekends, for delivery to a location of their choice.

The arrival of Subway on the third party apps follows in the footsteps of other favourites including KFC and Burger King, which both joined Just Eat last year.

*correct as of January 2020.

(Adapted from: https://www.subway.com/PressReleases/Subway%20trials%20delivery%20with%20Just%20Eat.pdf and https://www.subway.com/en-GB/AboutUs/SocialResponsibility/NutritionalLeadership)

Set 1 Paper 2

4 (a) Outline **one** benefit to *Subway* of behaving ethically. (2)

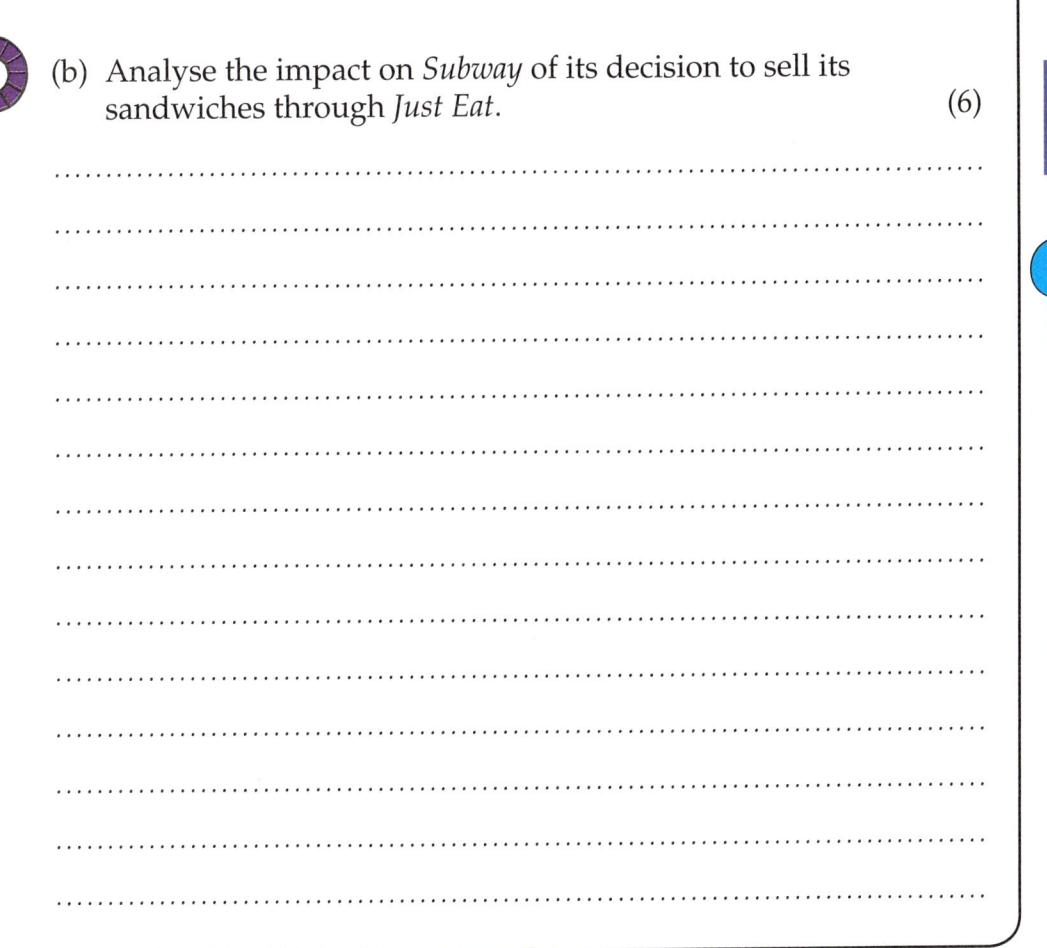

....

....

Revision Guide Page 57

Hint

'Outline' questions require you to make a valid **point** and to support it with **one linked strand of development**, including language specific to the sandwich market.

(b) Analyse the impact on *Subway* of its decision to sell its sandwiches through *Just Eat*. (6)

....
....
....
....
....
....
....
....
....
....
....
....
....
....

Revision Guide Page 65

Watch out!

Take care to check what the question is asking you to analyse. Here you are being asked to 'Analyse the impact', so you will need to discuss the benefits, the drawbacks or a combination of both, as impacts can be positive or negative. If you are taking a two-paragraph approach (analysing two points) then you can discuss either two benefits of selling through *Just Eat*, or two drawbacks, or one benefit and one drawback. All these options are valid.

(Total for Question 4 = 8 marks)

Approaching the question

In question 4b you are marked in two skills areas: **Application** and **Analysis**.

For **Application**, your answer needs to be relevant to *Subway* and *Just Eat* throughout, for example referring to 'sandwiches', 'fast food', 'takeaway delivery' and 'rival businesses'.

For **Analysis**, you must have at least five linked strands of development across your one or two points. Signal these with connectives such as 'therefore', 'this leads to' and 'this means that'.

5   Figure 3 shows the number of outlets and total revenue for the top 10 UK restaurant operators in 2017.

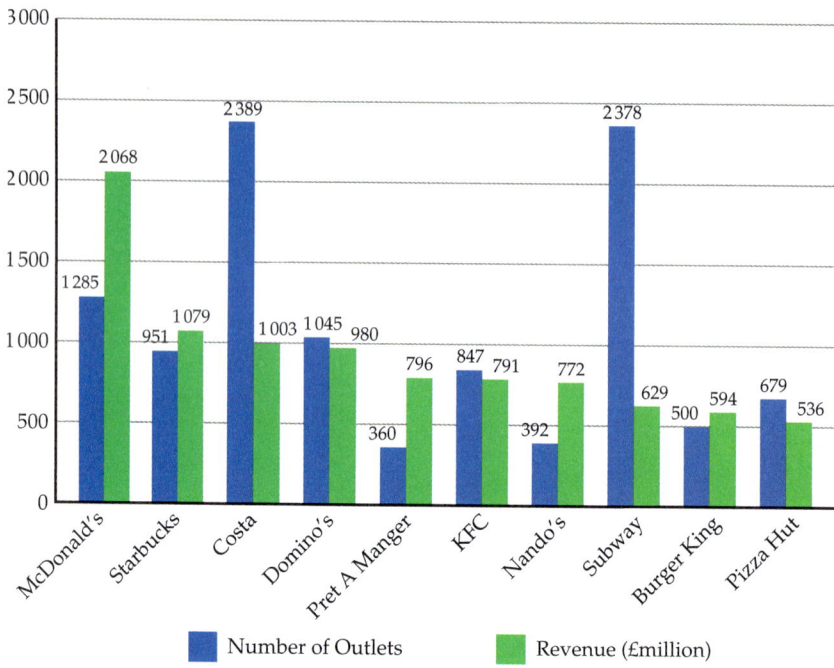

Figure 3

(a) Using the information in Figure 3, calculate the average revenue, to the nearest pound, per *Subway* outlet in 2017. You are advised to show your workings. (2)

£ ....

Revision Guide Page 88

Watch out!

Always check the units on the axis of a graph. For this question, the revenue is shown in £ million, so you need to be careful when calculating your answer.

(b) Using the information in Figure 3, calculate, to two decimal places, *Subway's* revenue as a percentage of the total market revenue of the top 10 restaurants. You are advised to show your workings. (2)

.... %

Revision Guide Page 88

Hint

This calculation requires you to use the revenue data only – make sure you use the right information from the graph.

Watch out!

If a 'Calculate' question asks you to give your answer to two decimal points, you must do this or you will lose marks.

Set 1 Paper 2

Revision Guide Page 67

Subway uses a system of job production to make each sandwich.

(c) Analyse the benefit to *Subway* of using job production. (6)

....
....
....
....
....
....
....
....
....
....
....

(Total for Question 5 = 10 marks)

LEARN IT!

Job production is where there is one-off production of a one-off item for a single customer, i.e. each sandwich is made to the customer's specific requirements.

Hint

Often, the benefits of one type of production method, for example job production, are the drawbacks of the opposite method of production, for example flow production.

Approaching the question

To demonstrate **Analysis**, you need to give one or two clear points and a minimum of five linked strands of development.

To demonstrate your skills in **Application**, your answer must be specific to *Subway*. You could use phrases such as 'fast food outlet', 'sandwich chain' and 'pre-packed sandwich'.

6 (a) State **one** benefit to *Subway* of having more than 42 500 locations worldwide. (1)

....

....

(b) Outline the drawback to *Subway* of using quantitative data to help make decisions. (2)

....

....

....

....

Set 1 Paper 2

Revision Guide Page 77

LEARN IT!

Centralised decisions are made by senior managers (normally at head office). Decentralised decisions are delegated to regional employees at local stores and branches.

Watch out!

When answering a 'Justify' question, to gain marks for **Application** you must apply your knowledge to the context of the case study. This means you need to refer to 'the sandwich chain', 'fast food outlets', 'restaurant managers', etc., throughout your response, including in the conclusion.

Currently *Subway* operates a centralised management system in its restaurants. To help it continue to be more competitive in the fast food restaurant market, *Subway* is considering the following two options.

Option 1: Continue with a system of centralisation for all outlets.

Option 2: Introduce a decentralised structure, giving autonomy to outlet managers.

(c) Justify which **one** of these two options *Subway* should choose. (9)

....
....
....
....
....
....
....
....
....
....
....
....
....
....
....
....
....
....
....
....
....
....
....
....
....
....

(Total for Question 6 = 12 marks)

TOTAL FOR SECTION B = 30 MARKS

Set 1 Paper 2

Approaching the question

In the 9-mark 'Justify' questions, you will always be given two options. There is no need to discuss both options.

Therefore, the simplest structure for answering this question is to focus on one option and adopt a three-paragraph approach.

- Paragraph 1: Make a judgement about which option you feel is best. Explain why you think this is. Aim to include at least three linked strands of development, so that you demonstrate **Analysis**. Make sure you refer to the context throughout, to demonstrate **Application**.

- Paragraph 2: State the drawback of the option you have chosen; this will help you show balance and count towards **Evaluation**. Aim to include at least three further linked strands of development.

(Remember, you need to have a minimum of five linked strands of development across your two points to gain top level Analysis, so by having six there will be no doubt that you have met this criterion.)

- Paragraph 3: Conclude your response by stating the main reason for your decision; in this case, why *Subway* should choose centralisation/decentralisation. Try to use the 'It depends' rule in your conclusion too, as you will gain extra credit for doing this successfully.

Ensure you refer to the context throughout to demonstrate **Application**. This means including language specifically related to the context of sandwiches and fast food.

SECTION C
Answer ALL questions.
Read the following extract carefully and then answer Question 7.
Write your answers in the spaces provided.

Makeup for men is becoming mainstream.

Chanel is a high fashion and beauty house that specialises in ready-to-wear clothes, luxury goods and fashion accessories.

The French fashion and beauty company is well-known for its extensive range of makeup for women, but in September 2018 it broke new ground by launching a makeup range aimed solely at men. Its new 'Boy de Chanel' range was launched with only a few products initially: an almost imperceptible lip balm, a tinted foundation, and an eyebrow pencil in various shades. These makeup products mark a new addition to the company's 'Boy' division, which has sold perfume and handbags for men since 2015.

As part of its launch, *Chanel* will conduct a product trial in South Korea (as this is the country with the highest demand and advancement in terms of makeup routines for men) before making them available on its website, www.chanel.com, and then eventually in *Chanel* stores worldwide.

When launching the product in Korea, *Chanel* will focus heavily on promotion and has lined up a famous Korean actor and model, Lee Dong Wook, to be the face of the 'Boy de Chanel' line. *Chanel* believes that this strategy of using celebrity endorsement will be particularly key to success when launching the product in Western markets. While this is a new venture for *Chanel*, other brands such as *Clinique* and *MMUK* already offer products designed for men, but by approaching specific celebrities to endorse its products, *Chanel's* may just be differentiated enough to have a competitive advantage.

(Source: *https://uk.fashionnetwork.com/news/Chanel-to-launch-a-line-of-makeup-for-men,1006103.html#.XGyTzfZ2uUk* and https://www.forbes.com/sites/tiffanyleigh/2018/08/27/chanel-debuts-boy-de-chanel-male-makeup-collection/#6c52ac8ee3c5)

7 (a) Define the term **product trial**. (1)

....
....
....

Chanel's sales for 2018 totalled $9.62 billion, which represented an 11 per cent increase from the previous year.

(b) Calculate, to two decimal places, the value of *Chanel's* sales in 2017. You are advised to show your workings. (2)

$ ....

(c) State **one** element of the sales process that will be important in helping *Chanel* provide a good level of customer service. (1)

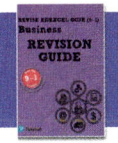

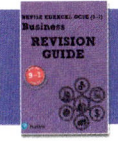

....
....
....

Set 1 Paper 2

Revision Guide Pages 84–85

Hint

Commission is a type of financial remuneration. Choosing the right remuneration method will maximise employees' productivity, whereas the wrong method could waste money and fail to provide any benefit. Also, money alone may not be enough to fully motivate employees; other needs, such as self-esteem, can be just as important in motivating staff.

LEARN IT!

Job enrichment develops employees' skills by giving them opportunities to lead, make key decisions and take on new responsibilities.

Hint

In your conclusion, use the 'It depends' rule to show that you recognise that there might be some circumstances where your chosen option may not be the most suitable.

To help its new makeup range to sell successfully, *Chanel* is considering two options to motivate its sales staff.

Option 1: Offering sales staff commission on the sales they make.

Option 2: Providing job enrichment by involving sales staff in the launch of the new range.

(d) Justify which **one** of these two options *Chanel* should choose. (9)

....
....
....
....
....
....
....
....
....
....
....
....
....
....
....
....
....
....
....
....
....

Approaching the question

'Justify' questions assess your skills in three areas: **Application**, **Analysis** and **Evaluation**.

Application: Your answer must be rooted in the context of *Chanel* throughout. In this question, referring to 'makeup', 'cosmetics', 'Clinique and MMUK', 'beauty products' and the actual products being launched will help you to achieve this.

Analysis: This is how well developed your response is. This question requires you to look at the benefit and drawback of one of the options. In doing so you need to have a minimum of five linked strands of development across your two points. It is best to aim for a minimum of three linked strands of development in each paragraph, in case one is not valid or is classed as repetition.

Evaluation: First, you must give a balanced response. This means recognising that an option has a drawback as well as a benefit. Avoid addressing only the benefit of each option. Giving a benefit of Option 1 and a drawback of Option 2 does not show balance but is a one-sided argument (a drawback of Option 2 only lends further support to Option 1).

Second, take time to conclude your response. You might consider: Why is the option you have chosen the best one? What is the key/vital reason in the context of *Chanel*?

Set 1 Paper 2

Revision Guide Page 66

LEARN IT!

The marketing mix refers to the 4 Ps of marketing, which are product, price, promotion and place.

Hint

To show the skill of **Analysis** throughout your answer, you should do the following.

- Ensure your answer has a minimum of **five linked strands of development**. These can be spread across the **two points** you make.
- Use connectives such as 'this means that', 'therefore' and 'this leads to' to help you achieve this.

(e) Evaluate whether promotion will be the most important component of the marketing mix in contributing to the successful launch of *Chanel's* new products. You should use the information provided as well as your knowledge of business. (12)

....

....
....
....
....
....

(Total for Question 7 = 25 marks)
TOTAL FOR SECTION C = 25 MARKS
TOTAL FOR PAPER = 90 MARKS

Set 1 Paper 2

Approaching the question

'Evaluate' questions are the only questions that test all four skill areas: **Knowledge and Understanding**, **Application**, **Analysis** and **Evaluation**.

Understanding: To demonstrate this skill, give clear definitions and use business terminology throughout your answer. While you are not required to start your response with a definition, it is a good habit to get into for 'Evaluate' questions. In this question you could define 'promotion' or 'marketing mix'.

Application: Throughout your response, you need to refer to *Chanel*, making your points specific to the case study, including in the conclusion. A good way of doing this is by referring to the specific makeup that *Chanel* sells rather than using a generic term such as 'products'.

Analysis: Make sure you have a minimum of five linked strands of development across the two points you make. Use connectives such as 'this would mean', 'therefore' and 'this leads to' to help you achieve this.

Evaluation: Aim to present a balanced argument. So, for this question, you might argue why promotion is the most important component, but you must also suggest why one of the other elements of the marketing mix is also important. You must also present a conclusion in which you discuss the main reason why your chosen element is the most vital.

Watch out!

To show the skill of **Application** throughout your answer, you should do the following.

- Refer to the makeup market and to *Chanel* itself, as well as to *Chanel*'s competitors, *Clinique* and *MMUK*.
- Use phrases from the case study such as 'makeup range', 'lip balm', 'eyebrow pencils', foundation, 'celebrity endorsement by Lee Dong Wook' and 'cosmetics firm'.

Hint

In your conclusion to this question, it would be wise to look at whether the success of *Chanel*'s new makeup range is actually due to a combination of elements rather than being reliant on any one component of the marketing mix in particular. You can use the 'It depends' rule to demonstrate this evaluative skill.

Set 2 Paper 1

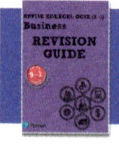

SECTION A

Answer ALL questions.

Write your answers in the spaces provided.

Some questions must be answered with a cross in a box ☒.
If you change your mind about an answer, put a line through the box and then mark your new answer with a cross ☒.

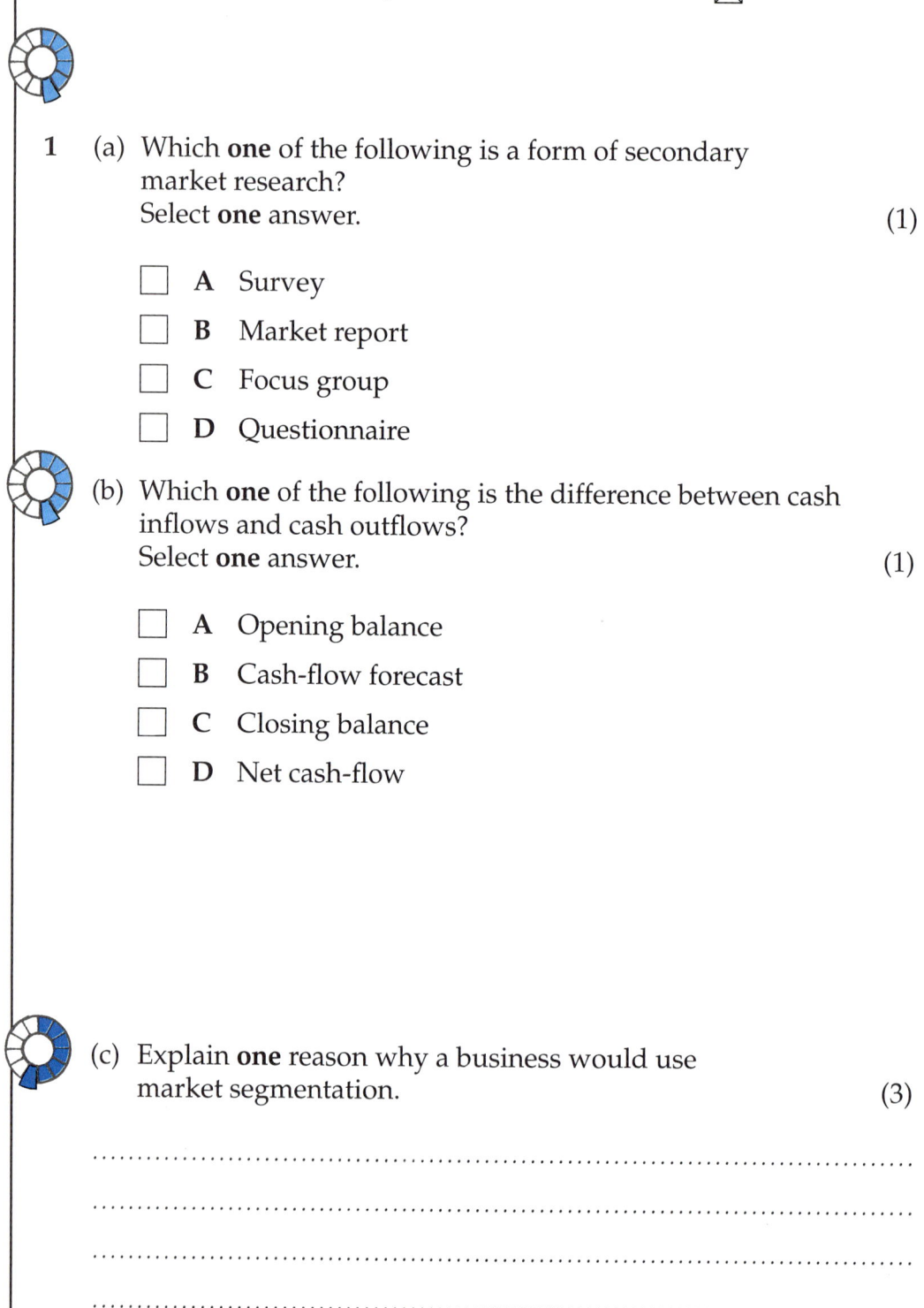

1 (a) Which **one** of the following is a form of secondary market research?
Select **one** answer. (1)

☐ A Survey

☐ B Market report

☐ C Focus group

☐ D Questionnaire

(b) Which **one** of the following is the difference between cash inflows and cash outflows?
Select **one** answer. (1)

☐ A Opening balance

☐ B Cash-flow forecast

☐ C Closing balance

☐ D Net cash-flow

(c) Explain **one** reason why a business would use market segmentation. (3)

....

....

....

....

....

....

....

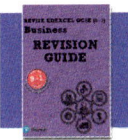

(d) Explain **one** benefit to a business if the interest rate is reduced.
(3)

....
....
....
....
....
....
....
....

(Total for Question 1 = 8 marks)

2 (a) Which **two** of the following are external influences on a business?
Select **two** answers. (2)

- [ ] **A** Market research
- [ ] **B** Exchange rate
- [ ] **C** Cash-flow
- [ ] **D** Limited liability
- [ ] **E** Unemployment

(b) Which **two** of the following are examples of short-term sources of finance?
Select **two** answers. (2)

- [ ] **A** Overdraft
- [ ] **B** Bank loan
- [ ] **C** Trade credit
- [ ] **D** Share capital
- [ ] **E** Retained profit

Set 2 Paper 1

Table 1 contains selected financial information for a business in March 2019. In that month, the business produced and sold 400 units.

Total fixed costs	£3 000
Total variable costs	£2 800
Price per unit	£15

Table 1

(c) Using the information in Table 1, calculate the break-even point for the business. You are advised to show your workings. (2)

.... units

Revision Guide Page 19

LEARN IT!

Break-even is the level of output at which a business's revenue covers its total costs.

Break-even point in units:

= $\dfrac{\text{Fixed cost}}{\text{Sales price} - \text{Variable cost}}$

Hint

You have been given the total variable costs for the month. You now need to work out the variable cost per unit by dividing total variable costs by the number of units.

Maths skills You may be awarded a calculation mark, even if the final answer you give is incorrect, so make sure you show all your workings as clearly as possible.

(d) Explain **one** reason why an entrepreneur might set up a business as a franchise. (3)

....
....
....
....
....
....
....

Set 2 Paper 1

Revision Guide Page 27

LEARN IT!

A franchise is the right given by one business (the franchisor) to other businesses (franchisees) to sell goods or services using its name, equipment and products. In return, the franchisee pays the franchisor a fee or share of the sales revenue. The franchisees remain independent businesses.

Hint

Consider the benefits of opening a franchise over other forms of ownership such as a sole trader or partnership.

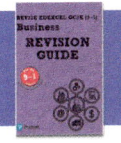

(e) Explain **one** way that employees could influence business activity. (3)

....
....
....
....
....
....
....

(Total for Question 2 = 12 marks)

Revision Guide Page 33

Hint

Think about one way this stakeholder group could influence the business's decision-making. Then give **two linked strands of development** to develop your point. Use connectives such as 'this means that' and 'therefore' to show your links.

Set 2 Paper 1

Revision Guide Page 37

LEARN IT!

Employment law governs all aspects of how a business interacts with its employees. Its purpose is to protect employees. Examples include the Health and Safety at Work Act 1974, Equality Act 2010, National Minimum Wage (Amendment) Regulations 2017 and Employment Relations Act 1999.

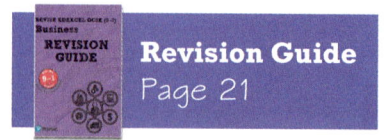

Revision Guide Page 21

Watch out!

Write your final answers on the answer spaces in Table 2. Remember to show your workings – as you may gain a mark for this even if your final answer is incorrect.

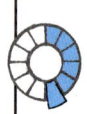

3 (a) Which **one** of the following is **not** covered by employment law? Select **one** answer. (1)

☐ A Recruitment
☐ B Product quality
☐ C Pay
☐ D Health and safety

Table 2 shows the cash-flow forecast for a small business.

	Apr (£)	May (£)
Cash inflow	....	7 000
Cash outflow	6 500	5 500
Net cash-flow	3 000	1 500
Opening balance	1 000	4 000
Closing balance	4 000	....

Table 2

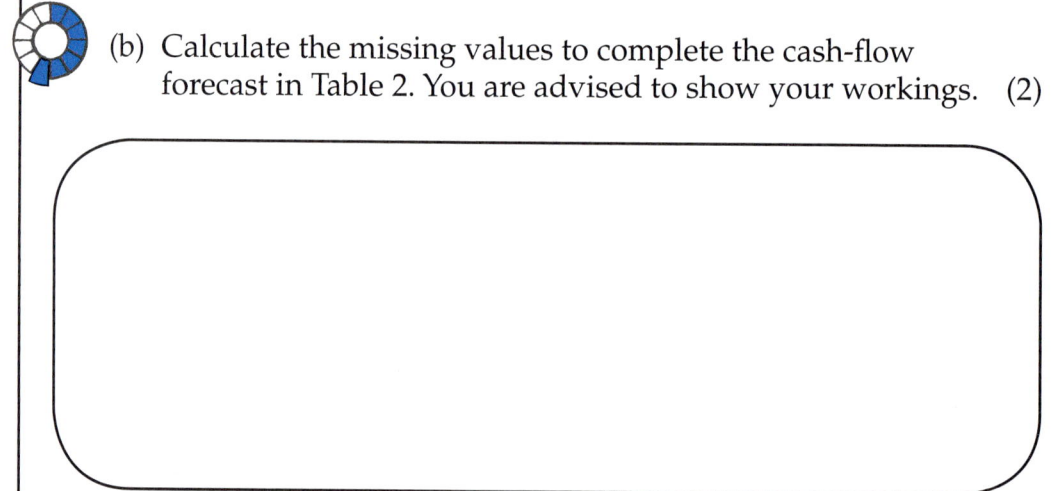

(b) Calculate the missing values to complete the cash-flow forecast in Table 2. You are advised to show your workings. (2)

46

(c) Explain **one** benefit to a business of being in close proximity to its market. (3)

....
....
....
....
....
....
....
....

Set 2 Paper 1

Revision Guide Page 28

Hint

A business's location – its proximity or nearness to various factors – is an important consideration. You need to explain one benefit of a business being located close to its market (its customers).

Watch out!

Make sure you fully read the question. Don't throw away marks by explaining a drawback when the question is asking for a benefit.

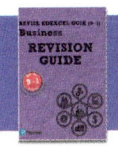

(d) Explain **one** benefit to a business of charging a high price for its products. (3)

....
....
....
....
....
....
....
....

Revision Guide Page 29

Hint

When answering a 3-mark 'Explain' question, you need to **make a point** (in this case, give an advantage) and then provide **two linked strands of development** using connective statements such as 'this leads to' and 'as a result'.

Set 2 Paper 1

Revision Guide Page 5

LEARN IT!

Entrepreneurs are risk-takers who have an initial idea and the willingness and confidence to see it through.

Hint

To answer this question, think about why entrepreneurs are important to the creation of a successful business. For example, you might mention their ability to organise resources and make business decisions, or their willingness to start new ventures and take risks.

(e) Discuss the role of entrepreneurship in setting up a successful business. (6)

....
....
....
....
....
....
....
....
....
....
....
....
....
....
....
....

(Total for Question 3 = 15 marks)

TOTAL FOR SECTION A = 35 MARKS

Approaching the question

When answering a 6-mark 'Discuss' question, you need to give one or two reasons supported by five linked strands of development. Use connectives such as 'this means that' and 'as a result' to show your links.

SECTION B

Answer ALL questions.

Read the following extract carefully and then answer Questions 4, 5 and 6.

Write your answers in the spaces provided.

After leaving college six years ago, Rob decided he had the skills and experience to set up his own gardening and landscape design business, *Down To Earth*, as a sole trader.

Rob had identified a gap in the market for a budget gardening service that could also offer a free garden design service. Many of the larger gardening companies Rob had come across charge a premium for detailed garden designs and consultancy. Rob planned to offer this service for free and use new technology to provide his customers with high-quality 3D designs of their new gardens.

Rob's market research into the local garden design and landscaping market found that there was little difference between competitors in terms of the service they provided. However, the largest competitor in the local area, *Olive Tree Gardens Ltd*, promoted its excellent customer service on its website.

In order to finance his own start-up, Rob estimated he would require £15 000. He invested £6 000 of his own savings and secured the remainder of the investment through a bank loan. As part of his application, Rob produced a detailed business plan.

In order that *Down to Earth* could establish a reputation for providing a premium service at a budget price, Rob decided to charge a price 25 per cent lower than the average competitor for *Down to Earth's* gardening and landscaping services.

Set 2 Paper 1

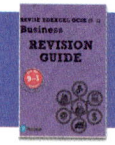

Revision Guide Page 32

Hint

Make sure your answer is specific to *Down to Earth*.

Revision Guide Page 26

Hint

An alternative approach for Rob to establish his business might have been to buy a franchise or set up as a private limited company. You could compare the option of a sole trader against either of these options.

Watch out!

In addition to explaining the advantages and/or disadvantages ('impacts' can be either) of setting up a business as a sole trader, you need to demonstrate Application in your answer – so make sure you refer to Down to Earth and the garden and landscape design market throughout your response.

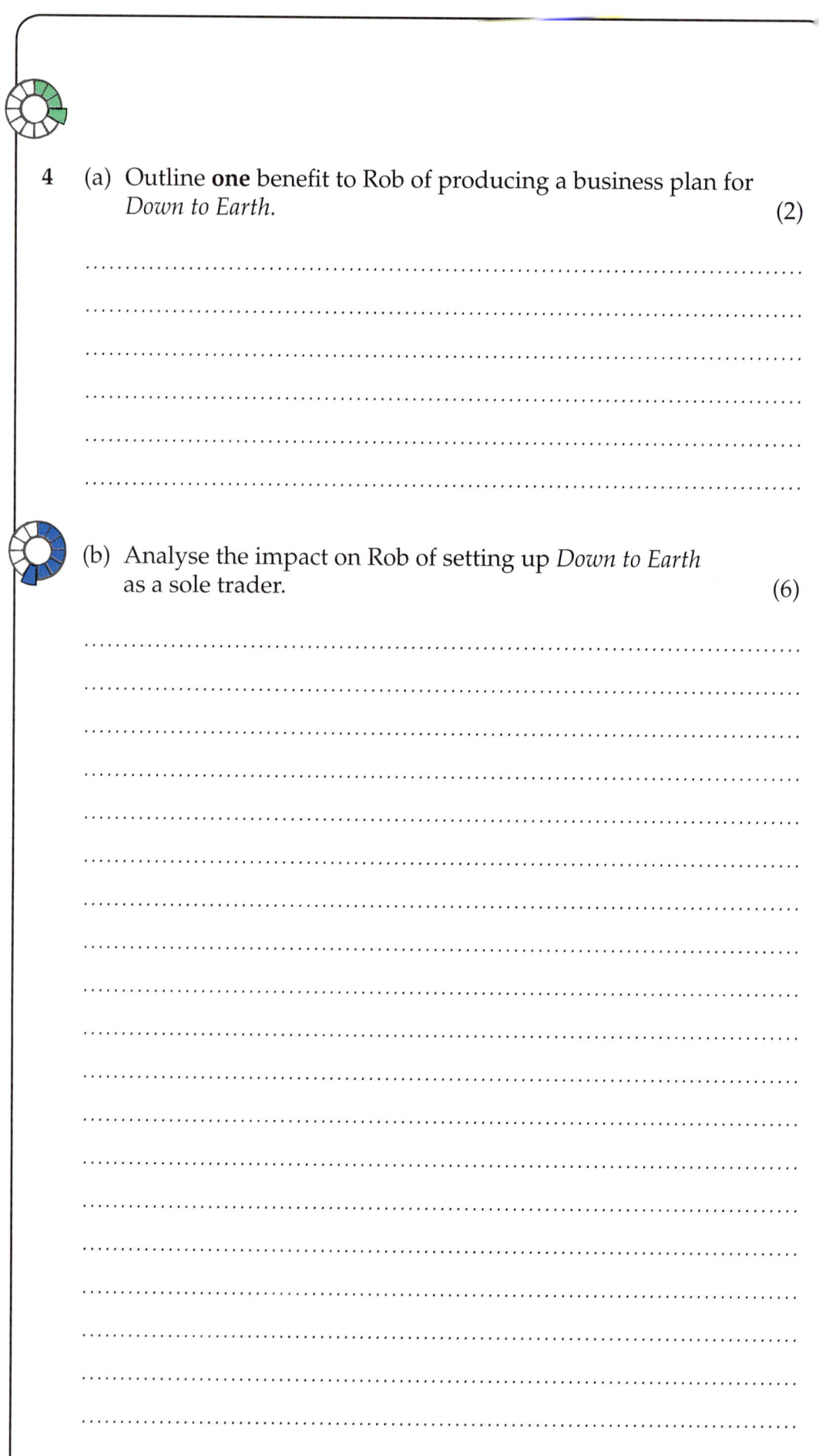

4 (a) Outline **one** benefit to Rob of producing a business plan for *Down to Earth*. (2)

……………………………………………………………………………………………………
……………………………………………………………………………………………………
……………………………………………………………………………………………………
……………………………………………………………………………………………………
……………………………………………………………………………………………………
……………………………………………………………………………………………………

(b) Analyse the impact on Rob of setting up *Down to Earth* as a sole trader. (6)

(Total for Question 4 = 8 marks)

50

5 Rob signed up his first customer in June. After the design service, Rob provided the customer with a materials estimate of £1 300 and a labour estimate of £1 500. In order to provide the customer with a final price, he needed to then apply the introductory discount of 25 per cent.

(a) Using the information above, calculate the total price after discount that the customer paid. (2)

£ ....

In July, Rob completed three garden projects for different customers. Table 3 shows *Down to Earth's* costs and revenue for that month.

Fixed costs	£400
Average variable costs per garden project	£700
Average revenue per garden project	£1 600

Table 3

(b) Using the information in Table 3, calculate the total profit Rob made in July. (2)

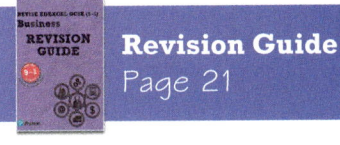

£ ....

Set 2 Paper 1

Revision Guide Pages 6–7

Hint

This question is asking you to 'Analyse the impact', so you can address either the benefits or the drawbacks (or one of each) for Rob of offering customers a 25 per cent discount – as impacts can be either positive or negative.

Hint

Giving customers a discount might attract potential customers, but it will make it harder for Rob to cover his business costs and achieve breakeven.

(c) Analyse the impact on *Down to Earth* of charging a price 25 per cent lower than the average competitor for the first six months. (6)

....
....
....
....
....
....
....
....
....
....
....
....
....
....
....
....

(Total for Question 5 = 10 marks)

Approaching the question

To demonstrate **Analysis** for this question, you need to give one or two clear points and a minimum of five linked strands of development. Remember to show **Application** to the *Down to Earth* context throughout. You can demonstrate this by using phrases from the case study such as 'gardening and landscape design business', 'budget gardening service' and 'detailed garden designs and consultancy'.

Set 2 Paper 1

6 (a) State **one** reason why Rob might have decided to start his own business. (1)

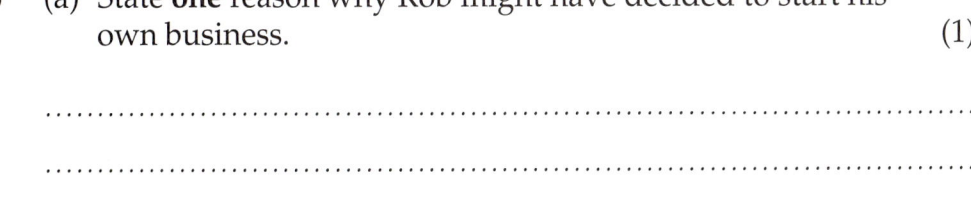

....
....

Revision Guide Page 2

Hint

Think about the potential rewards, for example personal satisfaction, financial success and the freedom to work independently.

Watch out!

'State' questions test **Application**.

(b) Outline **one** benefit to Rob of using new technology in his business. (2)

....
....
....
....
....
....

Revision Guide Page 35

Hint

'Outline' questions require you to make a valid point and then support it with one linked strand of development. Make sure your answer is specific to *Down to Earth*, for example by referring to garden software.

Hint

Think about how technology can improve customer service, promote a business or lower business costs.

Set 2 Paper 1

Rob is considering two options to increase revenue for *Down to Earth*.

Option 1: Advertise *Down to Earth* on the local radio.

Option 2: Give customers a £50 voucher if a recommendation from them leads to a new contract.

(c) Justify which **one** of these two options Rob should choose. (9)

Revision Guide Page 29

LEARN IT!

Promotion is communication between the business and customers that makes customers aware of the business's products. It includes advertising, sales promotions, sponsorship and public relations. It is one of the 4 Ps of the marketing mix (product, place, promotion, price).

Hint

Either option may increase Rob's business costs. However, you will have to decide which of the two options will lead to the biggest increase in the number of customers who use *Down to Earth*'s services.

....
....
....

(Total for Question 6 = 12 marks)

TOTAL FOR SECTION B = 30 MARKS

Set 2 Paper 1

Approaching the question

'Justify' questions examine three skills areas.

- **Application:** Applying your knowledge and understanding to the particular context. This means you should continually refer to the context throughout your response, including in the conclusion.

- **Analysis:** Developing your points by using examples and adding information. Your response must contain a minimum of five linked strands of development. Use clear connectives, such as 'this means that', 'this leads to' and 'because', to make your links clear.

- **Evaluation:** Writing a balanced argument that considers the benefit and drawback of a particular action. You must also make it clear what your chosen option is and your main reason for selecting that option. This will demonstrate that you can weigh up arguments. The best answers use the 'It depends' rule to demonstrate that you understand there are other factors that could change your decision.

Watch out!

You must give a balanced response to the 9-mark 'Justify' questions. This means recognising that an option has a drawback as well as a benefit. Avoid addressing only the benefit of each option. Giving a benefit of Option 1 and a drawback of Option 2 does not show balance but is a one-sided argument (a drawback of Option 2 only lends further support to Option 1).

SECTION C
Answer ALL questions.
Read the following extract carefully and then answer Question 7.
Write your answers in the spaces provided.

Rags to Riches manufactures unique bags and accessories from recycled materials. Martha set up the company five years ago when she ran the company from her home. *Rags to Riches* now employs three workers and operates from a small factory where the unique and one-off bags are designed and made.

Martha has always used social media to promote her brand. Every new product is shared on the company's Instagram account; customers can then follow a link to purchase the bag from the *Rags to Riches* website. *Rags to Riches* also sells a small proportion of its products through small independent retailers. Furthermore, 15 per cent of all revenue generated by *Rags to Riches* goes towards helping the homeless buy formal clothing for work.

Most of the materials used to make the bags come from recycled clothing. *Rags to Riches* purchases the clothing in bulk by the ton from collection and recycling companies in order to benefit from a discount on large volumes purchased. Using recycled materials in this way helps *Rags to Riches* to keep its variable costs low, but due to the large volumes purchased, some of the material is not suitable for the bags, with almost 30 per cent of the material going to landfill.

7 (a) State **one** fixed cost for *Rags to Riches*. (1)

....

....

Figure 1 shows *Rags to Riches'* financial data for 2015–2018.

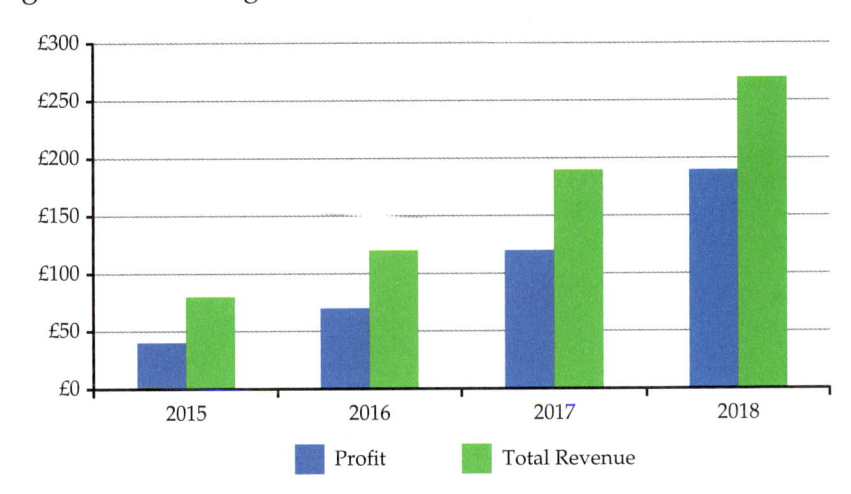

(b) Identify, using Figure 1, the year when *Rags to Riches'* profit was 50 per cent of total revenue. (1)

....

....

(c) Outline **one** benefit to *Rags to Riches* of manufacturing unique bags for its customers. (2)

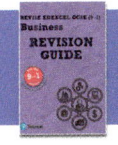

....

....

....

....

....

Set 2 Paper 1

Revision Guide Page 4

Hint

This question is about added value. Added value is the difference between the cost of producing each bag and how much customers are willing to pay. The key to answering this question is to analyse which option would be best at helping *Rags to Riches* increase its prices while maintaining or lowering its variable costs.

Martha has identified **two** ways that *Rags to Riches* could add value to its products.

Option 1: Improve the quality of each bag.

Option 2: Offer customers the option of having their initials embroidered on the bags.

(d) Justify which **one** of these two options Martha should choose.

(9)

Set 2 Paper 1

> **Approaching the question**

You must give a balanced response to the 9-mark 'Justify' questions. This means recognising that an option has a drawback as well as a benefit. Avoid addressing only the benefit of each option. Also, giving a benefit of Option 1 and a drawback of Option 2 does not show balance but is a one-sided argument (a drawback of Option 2 only lends further support to Option 1).

Before choosing which option you prefer, consider them both and how many points you could make. In this case, think briefly about improving quality and embroidering initials – which would appeal to the most customers and enable *Rags to Riches* to maximise their prices. What would be the drawbacks? Then choose just one of the options and write about the benefits and drawbacks of it and write your conclusion, using the 'It depends' rule.

Set 2 Paper 1

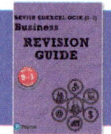

Revision Guide Pages 38, 41–42

Hint

You could start your answer by analysing how a rise in the price of second-hand clothing will lower the profits of *Rags to Riches*. You could then go on to compare this to other factors that are also significant in influencing the profits of *Rags to Riches* – for example, demand for its bags, the price it is able to charge its customers or the discount for bulk orders.

Hint

In your conclusion it is useful to apply the 'It depends' rule. The answer to a 12-mark 'Evaluate' question may depend on a factor not mentioned; for example, the extent to which the cost of second-hand clothing is likely to fluctuate or the value of the pound.

Many collection and recycling companies export second-hand clothing in bulk. Due to increased demand from abroad, the cost of buying second-hand clothing has increased by 15 per cent in the last 12 months.

(e) Evaluate whether the rising cost of recycled clothing will impact on the profits of *Rags to Riches*. You should use the information provided as well as your knowledge of business.

(12)

....
....
....
....

(Total for Question 7 = 25 marks)

TOTAL FOR SECTION C = 25 MARKS

TOTAL FOR PAPER = 90 MARKS

Approaching the question

'Evaluate' questions test all four skill areas.

Understanding: Give clear definitions and using business terminology throughout your answer.

Application: Refer to *Rags to Riches* throughout your response. A good way of doing this is by using specific words and phrases from the case study, such as 'unique and one-off bags' or 'accessories from recycled materials'.

Analysis: Include a minimum of five linked strands of development across the two points you make. Show your links using connectives such as 'this means that', 'therefore' and 'this leads to'.

Evaluation: Present a balanced argument. You must argue why the rising price of recycled clothing will impact on the profits of *Rags to Riches*, but you must also suggest why it may not why other economic factors may also play a significant role. Finally, give a balanced conclusion.

Set 2 Paper 2

SECTION A
Answer ALL questions.
Write your answers in the spaces provided.
Some questions must be answered with a cross in a box ☒.
If you change your mind about an answer, put a line through the box ☒ and then mark your new answer with a cross ☒.

Revision Guide Page 59

Hint

The design mix combines several elements that go into successfully planning a new product. The term 'aesthetics' can be used interchangeably with 'appearance'.

1 (a) Which **one** of the following is **not** an element of the design mix?
Select **one** answer. (1)

☐ **A** Cost
☐ **B** Function
☐ **C** Quality
☐ **D** Aesthetics

Revision Guide Page 59

LEARN IT!

The product life cycle shows the stages a product goes through from development to being withdrawn from sale.

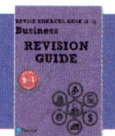

(b) Which **one** of the following is the phase of the product life cycle when sales will be maximised?
Select **one** answer. (1)

☐ **A** Growth
☐ **B** Maturity
☐ **C** Introduction
☐ **D** Decline

Revision Guide Page 56

Hint

You need to make **one valid point** (in this case you have to provide a suitable disadvantage of moving overseas) followed by **two linked strands of development**.

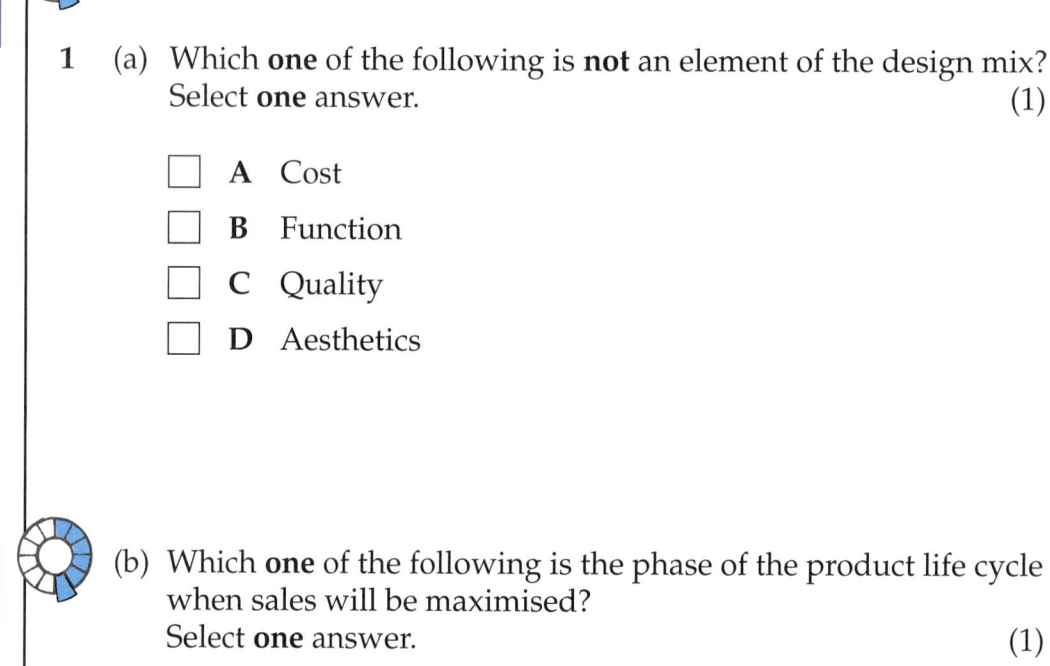

(c) Explain **one** drawback to a business of entering a new overseas market. (3)

....
....
....
....
....
....
....

62

(d) Explain **one** benefit to a business of using flexible working contracts for its employees. (3)

....
....
....
....
....
....
....
....

(Total for Question 1 = 8 marks)

Set 2 Paper 2

Revision Guide Page 79

LEARN IT!

A flexible working contract is a work agreement between a company and an employee that doesn't specify how many hours of work will be provided.

2 (a) Which **two** of the following are advantages to a business of flow production?
Select **two** answers. (2)

- ☐ **A** Provides an identical product each time
- ☐ **B** Production is flexible, therefore able to meet individual customer needs
- ☐ **C** Highly cost-effective, as production can be fully automated
- ☐ **D** Can get some cost advantages while still offering variations of a product
- ☐ **E** Low set-up costs

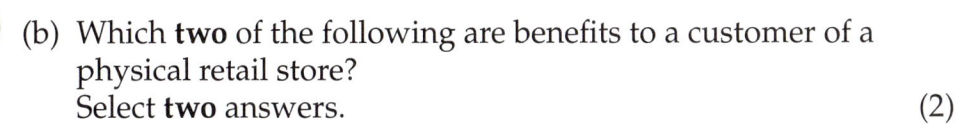

(b) Which **two** of the following are benefits to a customer of a physical retail store?
Select **two** answers. (2)

- ☐ **A** Customers can visit at any time of the day
- ☐ **B** There are always less costs involved for the business, so prices are cheaper
- ☐ **C** It is much easier to make price comparisons compared with online retailing
- ☐ **D** The customer gets the product immediately
- ☐ **E** Customers get to touch and see the actual product prior to buying, making it easy to compare it with other products

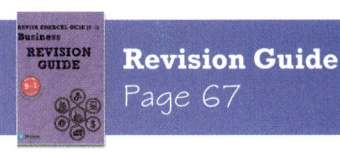

Revision Guide Page 67

LEARN IT!

Flow production is continuous production of identical products, which makes it suitable for high levels of automation, for example the manufacture of milk bottles.

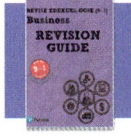

Revision Guide Page 65

LEARN IT!

A retailer is a shop or chain of shops, typically selling from a building in a high street or shopping centre. An e-tailer is a firm that sells via e-commerce or mobile commerce.

63

Set 2 Paper 2

Table 1 contains some information about a business.

Sales revenue	£598 000
Gross profit	£368 000
Other operating expenses and interest	£296 000

Table 1

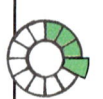

(c) Using the information in Table 1, calculate the net profit for the business. You are advised to show your workings. (2)

£ ....

Revision Guide Page 73

LEARN IT!

Net profit is the profit that a business can return to shareholders (owners) or reinvest back into the business.

Maths skills The units will always be given to you (here £ is given in the answer line). Make sure you put your final answer on the line provided, so it is clear what your response is.

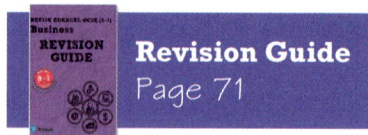

Revision Guide Page 71

(d) Explain **one** drawback to a business of producing and selling a high-quality product. (3)

....
....
....
....
....
....
....

Watch out!

Make sure you fully read the question. Don't make the mistake of fully explaining a benefit when the question is asking for a drawback.

Set 2 Paper 2

(e) Explain **one** drawback to a business from increased globalisation. (3)

....

....

....

....

....

....

....

(Total for Question 2 = 12 marks)

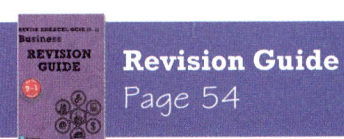

Revision Guide Page 54

LEARN IT!

Globalisation is the process by which businesses start to operate on an international scale.

Hint

You need to make **one valid point** (in this case you have to provide a drawback of globalisation on a business) followed by **two linked strands of development**, using connectives such as 'therefore', 'this leads to', 'because' and 'this means that'.

---

3 (a) Which **one** of the following is an external source of finance? Select **one** answer. (1)

☐ **A** Retained profit
☐ **B** Share capital
☐ **C** Selling assets
☐ **D** Sales revenue

Revision Guide Page 54

LEARN IT!

External sources of finance are when a business raises money from outside the organisation.

65

Set 2 Paper 2

Figure 1 shows the profit for Business A between September and December 2018.

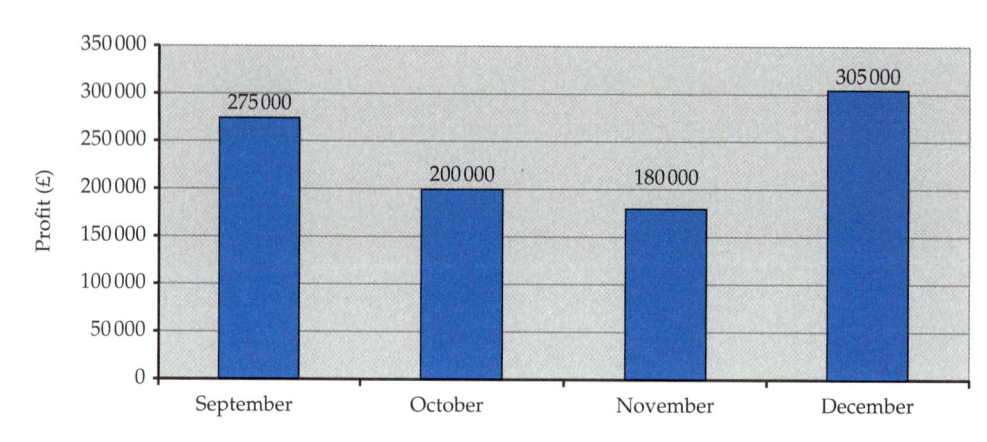

Bar chart (Profit £):
- September: 275 000
- October: 200 000
- November: 180 000
- December: 305 000

Figure 1

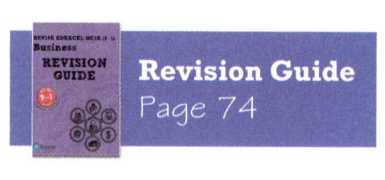

(b) Using the information in Figure 1, calculate the average monthly profit for Business A for the four months between September and December 2018. You are advised to show your workings. (2)

£ ....

Revision Guide Page 74

Maths skills In the exam you will have to do some mathematical calculations. These could include calculating the percentage increase or decrease of a figure or – as in this question – working out an average.

Watch out!

Always show your workings clearly. Even if you give an incorrect answer, you may be awarded 1 mark for correct calculation.

(c) Explain **one** benefit to a business of providing sponsorship. (3)

....
....
....
....
....
....
....

(d) Explain **one** method that a business might use to help ensure it provides good customer service. (3)

....
....
....
....
....
....
....

Set 2 Paper 2

Revision Guide Page 63

Hint

Think about why companies would want to spend large amounts of money to associate their name with events such as sport and concerts – how do they benefit?

Watch out!

Read the word that follows 'one' carefully – sometimes it could be 'drawback' or 'method' or 'way', which would make the question totally different. Here it is 'benefit'.

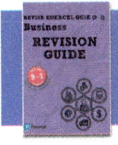

Revision Guide Page 72

Watch out!

When a question asks you to explain 'a method', make sure you do not make the mistake of explaining a benefit or drawback, as this will not gain you any marks. In this question you must explain **how** the business provides good customer service rather than the benefit of having good customer service.

Set 2 Paper 2

Revision Guide Page 77

LEARN IT!

A hierarchy is a structure of different levels of authority in a business organisation, one on top of the other. A business with a hierarchical structure has a long chain of command. This makes the business easier to control and provides opportunities for promotion, but it can be costly and slow down effective communication.

(e) Discuss the impact to a business of having a hierarchical structure. (6)

....
....
....
....
....
....
....
....
....
....
....
....
....
....

(Total for Question 3 = 15 marks)

TOTAL FOR SECTION A = 35 MARKS

Approaching the question

This question asks you to 'Discuss the impact'. Impacts can be positive or negative, so you could answer this question in different ways. For example, you could discuss one impact or two impacts.

If you choose to discuss two different impacts, you could discuss: two benefits or two drawbacks, or one benefit and one drawback.

Make sure you have at least five linked strands of development across the point(s) you make.

SECTION B

Answer ALL questions.

**Read the following extract carefully and then answer Questions 4, 5 and 6.
Write your answers in the spaces provided.**

The budget hotel chain *Travelodge* has announced it will be opening six new hotels in the UK. This represents an investment of £45 million in the new hotels, bringing the total number of *Travelodge* hotels in the UK, Ireland and Spain to 595 in 2020. The six new hotels will also create an additional 135 jobs.

In Edinburgh, the new hotel will be a *Travelodge PLUS*, which the company calls its 'budget chic' format. *Travelodge PLUS* hotels include king-size beds, blackout curtains, bespoke wall art and a new-look restaurant. They feature *Travelodge* 'SuperRooms™' which each offer a *Lavazza* coffee machine, hypoallergenic pillows, a three-jet shower and 32" *Samsung Freeview* TV. Following feedback from customers, *Travelodge PLUS* hotels are designed to appeal to budget travellers who want a touch of luxury.

However, the company still has a strong focus on budget to help them compete with rivals such as *Premier Inn*. Rooms are on offer from £29 per night, and dinner deals from £12.25, with special offers for families, such as children eating free.

Travelodge continues to have a strong online presence, receiving more than a million visits a week to its website. It uses appealing discounts to compete with other online sites such as *Booking.com* and *Expedia*.

Set 2 Paper 2

Revision Guide Page 50

Hint

In 'Outline' questions, make a valid point (in this case, one drawback of selling their service cheaply) with one linked strand of development. You also need to apply your answer to *Travelodge*.

Revision Guide Page 60

4 (a) Outline **one** drawback to *Travelodge* of being a budget hotel chain. (2)

....
....
....
....

(b) Analyse the benefit to *Travelodge* of launching *Travelodge PLUS*. (6)

....
....
....
....
....
....
....
....
....
....
....
....
....
....
....
....

(Total for Question 4 = 8 marks)

Approaching the question

'Analyse' questions require a similar structure to 'Discuss' questions. You can answer them by making **one point** and then having **five linked strands of development** across that point, or by making two points and then having five linked strands of development across those two points.

5 Figure 2 shows information relating to *Travelodge's* revenue for 2018.

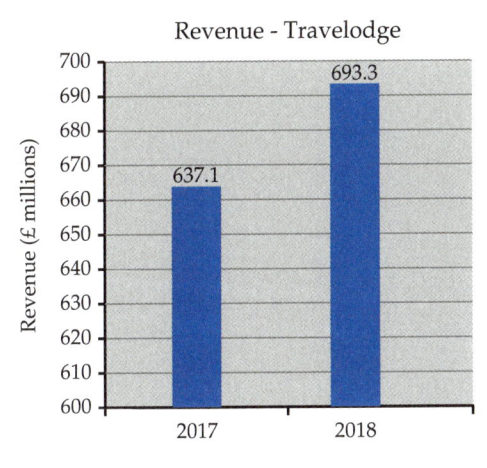

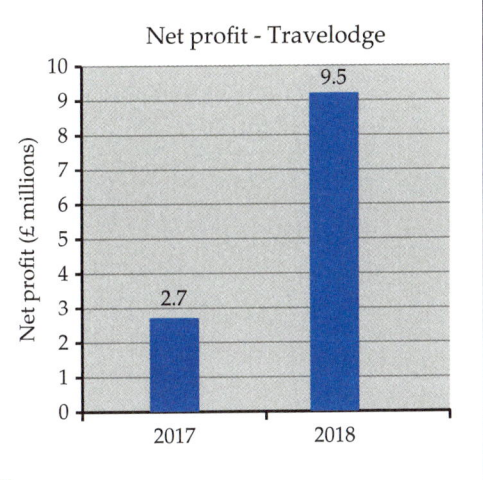

Figure 2

(*Data source:* https://www.travelodge.co.uk/sites/default/files/T&L_2018_signed_accounts.pdf)

(a) Using the information in Figure 2, calculate, to two decimal places, the percentage change in *Travelodge's* revenue between 2017 and 2018. You are advised to show your workings. (2)

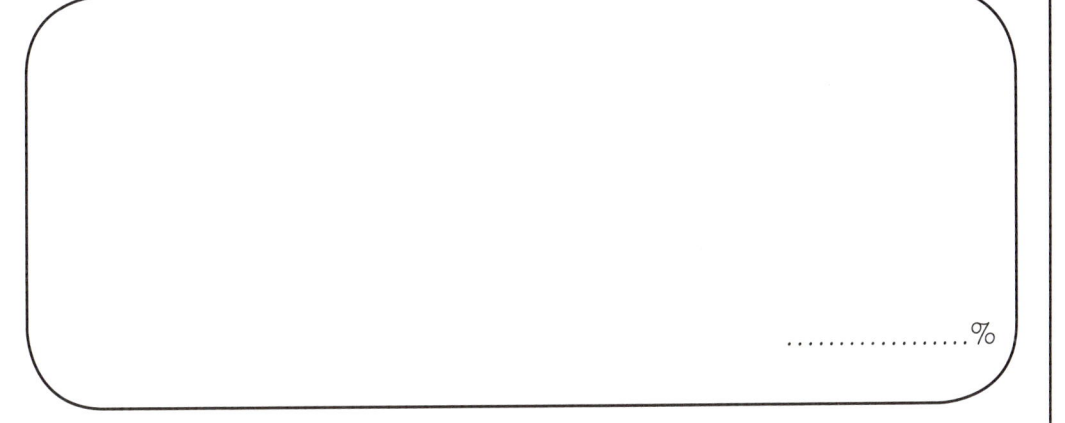

.................%

(b) Using the information in Figure 2, calculate, to two decimal places, *Travelodge's* net profit margin in 2018. You are advised to show your workings. (2)

.................%

Set 2 Paper 2

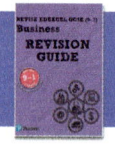

Revision Guide Page 65

Watch out!

Make sure your answer gives an impact on the business and not on the customer. Many students would be tempted to write about the level of convenience for the customer but this is not what the question is asking for.

Hint

With 'Analyse' questions, you will be marked in two skill areas; **Application** and **Analysis**. To gain **Application** marks your answer needs to be specific to *Travelodge*. For instance, writing 'One benefit is that the business will not need as many stores' shows understanding but is **not** applied to this business since *Travelodge* doesn't have stores. Instead you could write, 'One benefit is that the hotel chain will not need as many telephone agents to sell rooms'. In this example, 'Hotel chain' and 'telephone agent' would count as context. You need to use context throughout.

(c) Analyse the impact on *Travelodge* of selling through its website.
(6)

....
....
....
....
....
....
....
....
....
....
....
....
....
....
....
....

(Total for Question 5 = 10 marks)

6 (a) State **one** piece of market data that *Travelodge* may have considered when deciding whether to build a *Travelodge PLUS* in Edinburgh. (1)

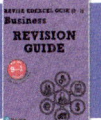

....
....

(b) Outline **one** reason why it is important that *Travelodge* responds to customer feedback. (2)

....
....
....
....

Set 2 Paper 2

To finance further *Travelodge PLUS* hotels, *Travelodge* is considering the following two options.

Option 1: Borrow more money from banks.

Option 2: Sell assets.

(c) Justify which **one** of these two options *Travelodge* should choose.

(9)

Revision Guide Page 51

Hint

A large business may sell assets that it no longer needs, such as fixed assets (e.g. machinery) or excess stock. This is a quick way of raising capital, but the business loses the benefit of owning the assets that it sells.

LEARN IT!

Loan capital is when a long-term bank loan is secured against the business's assets. Interest will be charged and the business will have to make fixed repayments to repay the debt.

....
....
....

(Total for Question 6 = 12 marks)

TOTAL FOR SECTION B = 30 MARKS

Approaching the question

'Justify' questions examine three skills areas.

- **Application:** Applying your knowledge to the particular context. This means you should **continually refer to the context** – travellers, rooms, budget chic, etc. You need to refer to this throughout your response, including in the conclusion.

- **Analysis:** Developing your points by using **examples and adding information**. Your response must contain a minimum of five linked strands of development. Use clear connectives, such as 'this means that', 'this leads to' and 'because', to make your links clear.

- **Evaluation:** Writing a **balanced argument** that considers the **benefit** and **drawback** of a particular action. You must also make it **clear what your chosen option** is and what your **main reason** is for selecting that option. This will demonstrate that you can weigh up arguments. The best answers use the **'it depends'** rule.

Set 2 Paper 2

75

SECTION C

Answer ALL questions.
Read the following extract carefully and then answer Question 7.
Write your answers in the spaces provided.

Primark is a fashion retailer that offers a varied range of products, including children's clothing, men's wear, women's wear, homeware, accessories, beauty products and confectionery. *Primark* now has over 350 stores in 11 countries across Europe and America.

One country *Primark* operates in is bargain-hunting Germany, where it plans to open two more stores in the next year as part of its growth strategy. This move abroad has been successful for *Primark*, as German shoppers favour good quality at a low price, something that has become synonymous with *Primark*.

Primark has also recognised the need to improve its ethical stance and as such has emphasised its commitment to environmental standards and safer working conditions, as it fights for market share. German customers demand high ethical standards and the retailer has started to display 'Primark Cares' posters in its German stores. These contain information about its factories and how it sources raw materials. As *Primark* does not manufacture its own products, it must be very selective about the factories it works with to maintain both quality for its customers and decent working conditions and wages for the factory workers. It achieves this by requiring every supplier to agree to achieving internationally-recognised standards, which it sets out in the *Primark* Code of Conduct. In addition, each factory is audited by an Ethical Trade and Environmental Sustainability Team, which comprises more than 100 experts who are based in key sourcing countries and who monitor compliance against *Primark's* Code. This procurement is key to *Primark's* success.

Primark faces strong competition from another discount retailer, *H&M*. Recently *Primark* has been successful in drawing customers away from its Swedish rivals. However, *H&M* is also putting a bigger emphasis on sustainability. As concerns about environmental impact are increasingly at the front of customers' minds, both *H&M* and *Primark* are promoting recycling and improved cotton-farming methods.

(References: https://www.businessoffashion.com/articles/news-analysis/primark-sharpens-ethical-focus-in-fight-for-market-share and https://www.primark.com/en/our-ethics/newsroom/2018/primark-expands-sustainable-cotton-programme-into-second-major-sourcing-country*)*

Set 2 Paper 2

Revision Guide Page 70

7 (a) Define the term procurement. (1)

....

....

Figure 3 shows the market share of major clothing retailers in the UK in 2008 and 2018.

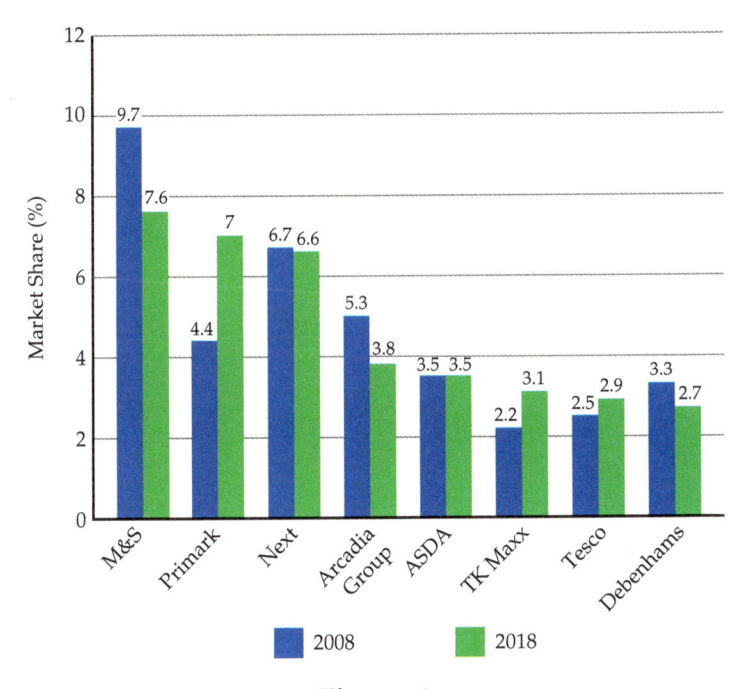

Figure 3

(Adapted from: https://www.just-style.com/news/ms-perilously-close-to-losing-top-clothing-retailer-spot_id133576.aspx)

(b) Using Figure 3, identify the retailer that achieved the greatest increase in market share between 2008 and 2018. (1)

....

....

Revision Guide Pages 75–76

Watch out!

This 'identify' question is NOT asking you to do any calculations – if the question required you to do a calculation, it would give the instruction 'Calculate' and there would be a box for working out and a space for recording the answer. You simply need to look at the graph and decide which company grew the most based on the height of the bar for 2018 compared to the height of the bar for 2008.

77

Set 2 Paper 2

Revision Guide Page 56

Hint

When answering questions that carry **Application** marks, such as this, go back and check the case study for the answer.

Watch out!

While the question asks for one reason, there are 2 marks available – so you need to give one reason then explain it, making sure your answer is linked to the case study.

(c) Outline **one** reason why *Primark* has chosen to open stores in Germany. (2)

....
....
....
....
....
....

To improve its competitiveness against other fashion retailers, *Primark* is considering the following two options.

Option 1: Concentrate on keeping prices lower than competitors.

Option 2: Improve its ethical standards.

(d) Justify which **one** of these two options *Primark* should choose.

(9)

....

**Set 2
Paper 2**

Revision Guide
Pages 57 and 61–62

Hint

In a 9-mark 'Justify' question, you do not need to refer to both options.

Hint

See overleaf for guidance on approaching this question.

79

Set 2 Paper 2

Hint

Remember, the 'It depends' rule is an important way to help you score highly for **Evaluation**. Once you have stated your conclusion, consider additional factors that might influence the decision, introducing these with 'It depends' and explaining what the effect might be.

....
....
....

Approaching the question

A good way of structuring your response to this question is to have three clear paragraphs.

- Paragraph 1: Start by making a judgement: state which option you think is best. Then explain the benefits of that option. In doing so, aim to write three linked strands of development and support your explanations with direct references to the case study, to demonstrate **Application**.

- Paragraph 2: Now focus on the drawbacks of your chosen option. Again, aim to have three linked strands of development – so that across the two points you have reached the minimum of five linked strands of development to achieve good marks for **Analysis**. Continue to demonstrate **Application** by referring directly to the information in the case study.
By including three linked strands of development in both paragraphs, you can be more confident that you are covering the overall requirement of five linked strands of development for this answer.

- Paragraph 3: Now write your conclusion. Why is your chosen option the best one? What is the crucial reason? What might it depend on? Remember that your conclusion must also continue to demonstrate **Application** by referring directly to the context of the case study.

(e) Evaluate whether *Primark's* relationship with its suppliers is the key factor in determining the profitability of the business. You should use the information provided as well as your knowledge of business. (12)

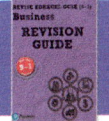

Set 2 Paper 2

LEARN IT!

Profitability is the degree to which a business is able to generate profit from its activities.

....
....

(Total for Question 7 = 25 marks)
TOTAL FOR SECTION C = 25 MARKS
TOTAL FOR PAPER = 90 MARKS

Hint

Once you have finished your answer, read back through it and highlight references to the case study. Ensure there are highlights throughout your answer to help you aim for high marks for **Application**.

Approaching the question

The best way to approach this question is using a three-paragraph structure.

- Paragraph 1: Explain why the relationship with *Primark's* suppliers is key to the company being profitable. Is *Primark's* profitability down to the quality of its supplies, or because the company can negotiate cheap prices for them? Ensure your paragraph has at least three linked strands of development and is fully applied to the case study.

- Paragraph 2: Now give a reason why *Primark's* relationship with its suppliers is not key to its profitability. In doing so, is there something else that is more critical to the company's success? Again, ensure your paragraph has at least three linked strands of development and is fully applied to the case study.

- Paragraph 3: Make the final paragraph your conclusion. Which side of the argument is stronger and why? What might your decision depend on? Make sure you use the case study to argue your point of view from *Primark's* perspective.

Set 3 Paper 1

SECTION A
Answer ALL questions.
Write your answers in the spaces provided.
Some questions must be answered with a cross in a box ☒.
If you change your mind about an answer, put a line through the box ☒ and then mark your new answer with a cross ☒.

1 (a) Which **one** of the following is a reward that an entrepreneur might expect to gain from running their own business?
Select **one** answer. (1)

☐ **A** Business failure
☐ **B** Independence
☐ **C** Financial loss
☐ **D** Lack of security

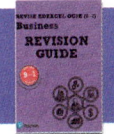

Revision Guide Page 2

Hint
Read through the different options carefully — some of them are risks rather than rewards.

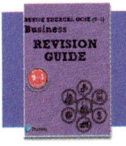

(b) Which **one** of the following is a **limitation** of market mapping?
Select **one** answer. (1)

☐ **A** Based on opinions and perceptions
☐ **B** Identifies potential gaps in a market
☐ **C** Identifies a business's closest rivals
☐ **D** Supports market segmentation

Revision Guide Page 12

LEARN IT!
A market map is a diagram that can be used to position and compare products in a market, to identify 'gaps' in the market (opportunities where customer needs are not being met) and the competition.

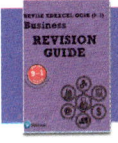

(c) Explain **one** way in which the local community is affected by a small business's activity. (3)

....
....
....
....
....
....
....
....

Revision Guide Pages 33–34

Hint
You could give a positive or a negative way; for instance, a small factory may give off a lot of pollution.

Set 3 Paper 1

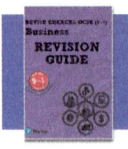

Revision Guide Page 9

LEARN IT!

Primary research (field research) is collecting information directly from a particular group of service users, such as a business's target market, for example via questionnaires, focus groups and surveys.

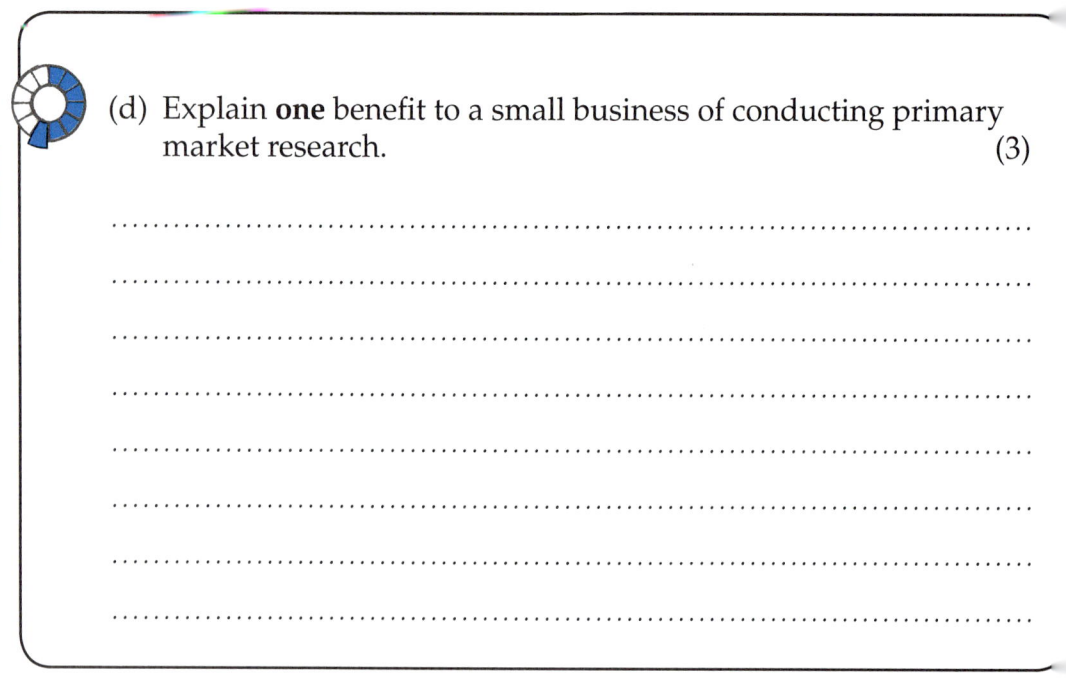

(d) Explain **one** benefit to a small business of conducting primary market research. (3)

....
....
....
....
....
....
....
....

(Total for Question 1 = 8 marks)

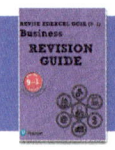

Revision Guide Page 11

LEARN IT!

A market segment is a group of customers who all share a similar characteristic; for example, age, lifestyle, gender, income or location.

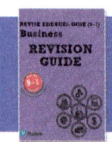

Revision Guide Page 41

Hint

If you were importing, would you now have to pay more or less for foreign goods? If you were exporting, would someone living abroad now have to pay more or less for your product?

2 (a) Which **two** of the following are benefits to a small business of segmentation?
Select **two** answers. (2)

☐ A Focusing on one group of customers means the business will not miss other opportunities

☐ B Targeting different customers with different products can be costly

☐ C The business will be able to attract a wide range of customers

☐ D The business will meet the specific needs of its customers

☐ E The business can target its marketing activities to the appropriate group of customers

(b) Which **two** of the following are most likely to happen as a result of a rise in the value of the pound compared to another currency?
Select **two** answers. (2)

☐ A Sales of UK exports fall as the price of exports goes up

☐ B UK firms sell more products abroad

☐ C UK importers suffer as imports become more expensive

☐ D UK residents are more likely to buy foreign imports as they have become cheaper

☐ E UK tourism flourishes as it is now cheaper for foreign tourists to come to the UK

Table 1 shows some financial information about a small business.

Selling price (£)	7.50
Fixed costs per year (£)	10 000
Variable cost per unit (£)	2.50
Number of units sold per year	15 000

Table 1

(c) Using the information in Table 1, calculate the number of units the small business needs to sell each year in order to break even. You are advised to show your workings. (2)

.... units

(d) Explain **one** way in which a small business can use technology to gain competitive advantage. (3)

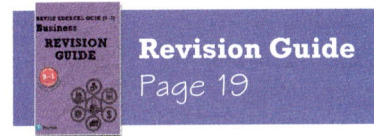

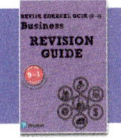

....
....
....
....
....
....
....

Set 3 Paper 1

Revision Guide Page 27

LEARN IT!

Franchise is the right, given by one business to another, to make, distribute or sell its branded goods or services. The franchisor is the business that licences this right; the franchisee is the business that makes, distributes or sells the branded product under the franchisor's name.

Watch out!

Make sure you learn key business terms and are clear how to use them correctly. For example, if you muddle the terms 'franchise', 'franchisor' and 'franchisee' in your answer to this question, you could lose marks.

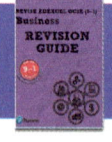

Revision Guide Page 29

Hint

The marketing mix is also known as the 4 Ps, but which of the 'Ps' in the question is not an element of the marketing mix? Read through the options carefully to find your answer.

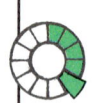

(e) Explain **one** drawback in setting up a small business as a franchise. (3)

....
....
....
....
....
....
....
....

(Total for Question 2 = 12 marks)

---

3 (a) A business is more likely to be able to charge a high price in which **one** of the following scenarios?
Select **one** answer. (1)

☐ **A** When a business has a lot of competitors

☐ **B** When a product has a reputation for having low quality compared to rivals

☐ **C** When a business launches an innovative product into the market

☐ **D** When a business aims its product at customers on low incomes

86

Figure 1 shows the net cash-flow for a business over three months.

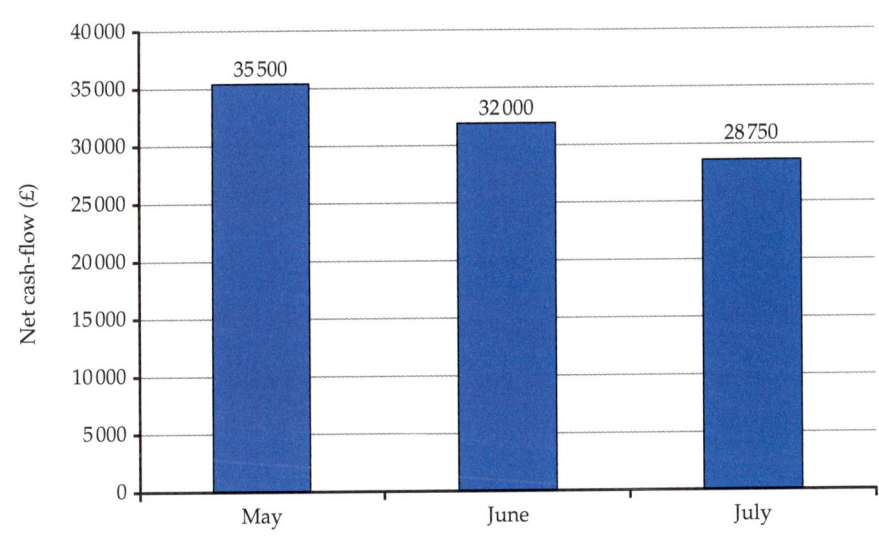

Figure 1

Net cash-flow (£) by month:
- May: 35 500
- June: 32 000
- July: 28 750

(b) Using the information in Figure 1, calculate, to two decimal places, the percentage decrease in the net cash-flow between May and July. You are advised to show your workings. (2)

.... %

Revision Guide Page 88

Maths skills

Calculating percentage decrease (or increase) is one of the key mathematical skills you might be asked to demonstrate in the exam. When calculating percentage change, you need to work out the difference between the two numbers, then divide this figure by the original number and multiply by 100.

Watch out!

Some calculation questions require you to give an answer to **two** decimal places, as this one does. If you do not follow this instruction you may lose a mark, even if your calculation is correct.

Set 3 Paper 1

87

Set 3 Paper 1

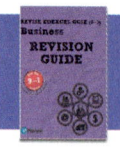

Revision Guide Page 13

Watch out!

This question is asking you to explain the **method** a business uses. In this case, make sure you explain a business process (for this question, a method of competing with rivals).

Hint

A business might assess the strengths and weaknesses of its competition using several criteria (for example, product range, customer service, quality or price) in order to differentiate its own products and services.

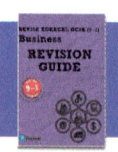

Revision Guide Page 40

Hint

A fall in interest rates will lower the cost of borrowing. Consider the effect on the money the business can spend, its cash flow, and ability to borrow money, and consumer spending. Explain one impact of this change on the business.

(c) Explain **one** method that a small business may use to compete with its rivals. (3)

....
....
....
....
....
....
....
....

(d) Explain **one** impact of a falling interest rate on a small business. (3)

....
....
....
....
....
....
....
....

88

Set 3 Paper 1

(e) Discuss the reason why cash is important to a small business.
(6)

....
....
....
....
....
....
....
....
....
....
....
....
....
....
....

(Total for Question 3 = 15 marks)

TOTAL FOR SECTION A = 35 MARKS

Revision Guide Page 22

Hint

Without sufficient cash, a business would be unable to:

- pay its suppliers and other debts
- repay bank loans
- pay wages to employees
- buy raw materials and products to sell
- promote the business.

You need to choose one or two of these reasons and analyse their impact on the business.

Approaching the question

'Discuss' questions can be answered using a one- or two-paragraph approach.

- If you decide on the one-paragraph approach, you will need to give just one reason why cash is important and support it with at least five linked strands of development.

- If you choose the two-paragraph approach then you will need to give two reasons why businesses need cash and support these with a total of at least five linked strands of development across the two points.

SECTION B

Answer ALL questions

Read the following extract carefully and then answer Questions 4, 5 and 6. Write your answers in the spaces provided.

Green Cars Ltd is an independent garage that offers car repairs and servicing. It is a family-run business (managed by Frank and his daughter, Megan) and has been trading for over 17 years. Throughout the years, *Green Cars Ltd* has retained its philosophy of traditional values, offering a personal, family service and affordable prices. The company is known for providing a high level of customer service.

After completing some market research, which included the creation of a market map, *Green Cars Ltd* decided to add a car sales division. This would involve purchasing second-hand cars it would then sell on. In order to do this, it needed to borrow money from the bank. Frank and Megan therefore put together a business plan, in order to convince the bank to lend them the money. While the bank manager agreed to the loan, she expressed concern that the current downturn in the economy could cause a drop in car sales, which would negatively affect the success of the new car sales division.

When *Green Cars Ltd* opened 17 years ago, it chose to locate in a small industrial estate on the outskirts of Chedgrave, a small village 10 miles southeast of Norwich. The owners are now considering whether a move to a location closer to a larger town, Beccles, would be more beneficial to the business now that the company is selling cars as well as repairing them. A site has become available in the centre of the town, but the rent for the site at Beccles is much higher than the current rent.

4 (a) Outline **one** drawback to *Green Cars Ltd* of being a private limited company. (2)

....
....
....
....
....
....

(b) Analyse the impact on *Green Cars Ltd* of borrowing money from the bank to fund the car sales division of the business. (6)

....
....
....
....
....
....
....
....
....
....
....
....
....
....

(Total for Question 4 = 8 marks)

Approaching the question

You can answer 'Analyse' questions in one of two ways:

- make one point with at least five linked strands of development
- make two points with at least five linked strands of development across those two points.

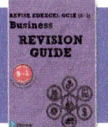

Set 3 Paper 1

Revision Guide Page 26

Hint

You need to make **a valid point**, with **one linked strand of development**. Your response must also be in the context of the *Green Cars Ltd* case study.

Revision Guide Page 24

Hint

You must use context throughout for 'Analyse' questions, in order to get top-level marks for **Application**. So, for this question, your answer must continually refer to the car business described in the case study. However, words that appear in the question cannot be used as context. For instance, in this question the term 'car sales' is used, so you would not gain any marks for Application when you use this term in your response – you would need to use alternative terms such as 'the garage' and 'second-hand car' business.

Set 3 Paper 1

Revision Guide Page 40

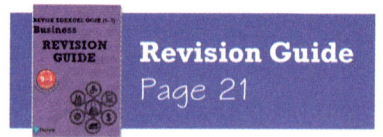

Maths skills Work out the annual interest, then calculate the interest charged for the whole ten-year period. (Remember that the business must pay back the original loan as well).

LEARN IT!

Annual interest = Loan amount × % rate

Total interest = Annual interest × Number of years

Revision Guide Page 21

LEARN IT!

Net cash-flow is the receipts of a business minus its payments.

You can calculate net cash-flow:

Cash inflows − Cash outflows in a given period

Maths skills Find the total payments by adding the fixed and variable payments before working out the net cash-flow.

---

5 In order to purchase second-hand cars for its new car sales division, *Green Cars Ltd* borrowed £125 000. It will repay the loan over 10 years. The interest rate the bank charges is 5 per cent per year.

(a) Calculate the total amount of money that will be repaid by *Green Cars Ltd* to the bank during the lifetime of the loan. You are advised to show your workings. (2)

£ ....

Table 2 shows the projected cash-flow information for *Green Cars Ltd* after taking out the bank loan.

Receipts	£275 000
Payment for fixed costs	£56 000
Payment for variable costs	£123 675

Table 2

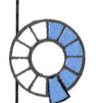

(b) Calculate the net cash-flow for *Green Cars Ltd*, based on the information shown in Table 2. You are advised to show your workings. (2)

£ ....

92

(c) Analyse the drawback that an economic downturn may have on *Green Cars Ltd*. (6)

....
....
....
....
....
....
....
....
....
....
....
....
....
....

(Total for Question 5 = 10 marks)

Set 3 Paper 1

Revision Guide Pages 38–39

Watch out!

This question asks you to analyse the drawback of an economic downturn for *Green Cars Ltd*. You will not be awarded any marks for analysing a benefit!

Approaching the question

'Analyse' questions are marked in two skill areas: **Application** and **Analysis**.

To gain marks for Application, you must use context throughout. For instance, for this question you would not gain any marks for Application by saying, 'One drawback is that customers may not purchase expensive products', as this does not reflect the content of the case study. To gain Application marks, you would need to write something like, 'One drawback is that the garage's customers may not purchase expensive cars and vehicles.'

93

Set 3 Paper 1

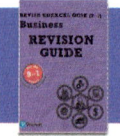

Revision Guide Page 31

Hint

'State' questions require you to give a short response, but it must be in context. In this case, just saying 'To help get the bank loan' would gain no marks.

Revision Guide Page 9

Watch out!

In 'Outline' questions many students only gain 1 of the 2 marks available. This is because they either forget to put their response into the context of the case study, or they fail to provide a linked strand of development. Remember: both are required to achieve the full 2 marks.

Hint

You have approximately two minutes to answer this question, so avoid wasting time by rewriting the question in your answer ('One benefit to Frank and Megan of *Green Cars Ltd* conducting primary research is that…'). Just give the answer in short sentences.

6 (a) State **one** reason why *Green Cars Ltd* decided to create a business plan. (1)

....

....

(b) Outline **one** benefit to Frank and Megan of *Green Cars Ltd* conducting primary research. (2)

....

....

....

....

....

....

Green Cars Ltd is considering two options with regards to its location, in order to try and improve future profitability.

Option 1: Remain in its current location on the industrial estate, where it has always been.

Option 2: Move to the new premises in the larger town of Beccles.

(c) Justify which **one** of these two options *Green Cars Ltd* should choose. (9)

....

(Total for Question 6 = 12 marks)

TOTAL FOR SECTION B = 30 MARKS

Set 3 Paper 1

Approaching the question

In 'Justify' questions, you only need to refer to one option in your answer. You can present a balanced argument using a three-paragraph approach.

- Paragraph 1: explanation as to why your chosen option is beneficial.
- Paragraph 2: explanation as to what the drawback of your chosen option is.
- Paragraph 3: conclusion: the main reason you have chosen the option you have and what the success of that option might depend on (the 'It depends' rule).

9-mark 'Justify' questions examine three skills areas: **Application**, **Analysis** and **Evaluation**.

Demonstrate **Application** by referring to the case study throughout the answer, including in the conclusion.

The best answers will demonstrate **Analysis** by including a minimum of five linked strands of development. Use clear connectives, such as 'this leads to' and 'therefore', to clearly demonstrate this skill.

Demonstrate **Evaluation** by writing a balanced argument that considers the benefits and drawbacks of the chosen option, and makes it clear what the main reason for selecting that option is. You should also aim to include a sophisticated evaluation technique, such as the 'It depends' rule.

SECTION C
Answer ALL questions.
Read the following extract carefully and then answer Question 7.
Write your answers in the spaces provided.

Baker's Dozen is a delicatessen shop and café serving homemade cooking, baking, specialities and freshly brewed coffee. It is a small business in the centre of the South Norfolk village of Loddon. The village is popular with tourists holidaying by boat on the nearby Norfolk Broads. In the village there are two other cafés – *Toffee Cake* (a rival upmarket café) and *Tim's Teas* (a more affordable option), both of which also target the tourist trade.

Baker's Dozen was set up as a partnership by three local women – Ashanti, Jo and Helen. The partners all want to bring a fresh style of café to the area by offering high quality, locally sourced produce. The women believe they have found a gap in the market, as there is no other local café with a deli shop (where people can buy food and drink to take home), but they didn't carry out any formal market research to determine this.

The café sells handmade pastries, sandwiches and cakes, all of which are made on the premises by the partners, who use high quality, locally sourced ingredients. The deli shop sells local cheeses, Italian meats and antipasti, as well as the more traditional pastries and cakes.

The partners decided the quality of the food and produce they sell should be reflected in the prices they charge. By the end of their first year of trading, they hadn't quite made the profit they had set themselves as an objective, so they decided to review the sales figures for both the café and the deli shop. In the café, the average spend by the 3750 customers they had that year was £12.00. The cost of making the food and drink they served them amounted to £5.50 and fixed costs for the café were £15 000.

Set 3 Paper 1

Revision Guide Pages 36–37

LEARN IT!
Legislation is the law that a business must comply with.

Hint
Your answer must also be in context – in this case, think about food hygiene.

Revision Guide Page 18

LEARN IT!
Total costs = Fixed costs + Variable costs

Watch out!
Write down the formula in order to help you remember it and apply the numbers during your calculation.

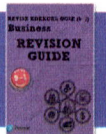

Revision Guide Page 4

Watch out!
Make sure you read the case study carefully to find the right answer.

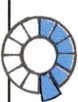

7 (a) State **one** impact that legislation may have on *Baker's Dozen*. (1)

....

....

(b) Using the information contained in the case study, calculate *Baker's Dozen's* total costs for the year. You are advised to show your workings. (2)

£ ....

(c) State **one** way in which *Baker's Dozen* has added value to the food it sells in the café. (1)

....

....

98

To make *Baker's Dozen* more competitive against its local rivals, the owners are considering the following two options.

Option 1: Charge lower prices in the deli counter and café sections, to be more comparable to competitors.

Option 2: Develop the deli counter further by providing a wider range of products.

(d) Justify which **one** of these two options *Baker's Dozen* should choose. (9)

....

Watch out!

When answering a 9-mark 'Justify' question, you don't need to refer to both options in your answer in order to gain all 9 marks, so just choose **one option** to write about.

In your first paragraph, explain the benefits of that option, and in the second paragraph explain the drawbacks of that option.

Don't make the mistake of explaining the benefit of the second option in your second paragraph, as this will not be a balanced argument.

Finally, use the third paragraph to write your conclusion, in which you explain the main reason why you have selected the option you have and consider what your decision might depend on.

Hint

See overleaf for guidance on how to approach 'Justify' questions.

Set 3 Paper 1

Approaching the question

You could adopt a three-paragraph approach when answering the 9-mark 'Justify' questions.

- Start paragraph 1 by making a judgement: should *Baker's Dozen* charge lower prices or develop their deli range in your opinion? You can choose either option. Explain why you think the option you selected is beneficial to *Baker's Dozen*. Include at least three linked strands of development and make your explanations relevant to the case study.

- In paragraph 2 explain the drawbacks of the same option, as this will help to show balance. Again, aim to have three linked strands of development. This will mean that, across the two paragraphs, you have sufficient linked strands to gain high marks for **Analysis**.

- Paragraph 3 is your conclusion, where you put the benefits and drawbacks into context. What is the main reason you have selected the option you have? What might it depend on?

(e) Evaluate whether the lack of detailed market research was the main reason why the owners of *Baker's Dozen* did not make as much profit as they expected. You should use the information provided as well as your knowledge of business. (12)

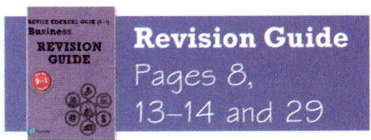

Set 3 Paper 1

....
....
....
....

(Total for Question 7 = 25 marks)

TOTAL FOR SECTION C = 25 MARKS

TOTAL FOR PAPER = 90 MARKS

Hint

To show the skill of **Analysis** throughout your answer, you should do the following.

- Ensure your answer has a minimum of five linked strands of development. These can be spread across the two points you make.
- Use connectives such as 'this means that', 'therefore' and 'this leads to' to help you achieve this.

Watch out!

To show the skill of **Application** throughout your answer, make sure you do the following.

- Refer to the café and food business, as well as *Baker's Dozen* competitors *Toffee Cake* and *Tim's Teas*.
- Use phrases from the case study such as 'fresh style of café', 'local café with a deli shop' and 'high quality, locally sourced produce'.

Approaching the question

The best way to approach the 12-mark 'Evaluate' question is using a three-paragraph structure.

- Paragraph 1: Start by offering a clear and concise definition of what market research is, to demonstrate **Knowledge and Understanding**. Then consider whether the lack of detailed market research could explain why *Baker's Dozen* did not make as much profit as anticipated. Did the partners misjudge the competition? Is there less demand for their products than expected? Ensure your paragraph has at least three linked strands of development and is fully applied to the case study.

- Paragraph 2: You now need to put forward an alternative reason why *Baker's Dozen* was not as successful as predicted. Is it because of a weak product offering? A lack of promotion? Poor customer service? As with the first paragraph, include at least three linked strands of development and reference the case study throughout. By including three linked strands of development in both paragraphs, you can be confident that you are covering the overall requirement of five linked strands of development for this answer.

- Paragraph 3: The final paragraph should be your conclusion. Justify what you think the main reason is for *Baker's Dozen* not making its profit targets – is it lack of market research or something else? Continue to refer closely to the case study to argue your point of view from *Baker's Dozen* perspective.

Set 3 Paper 2

SECTION A

Answer ALL questions. Write your answers in the spaces provided.

Some questions must be answered with a cross in a box ☒.
If you change your mind about an answer, put a line through the box ☒ and then mark your new answer with a cross ☒.

Revision Guide Page 77

1 (a) Which **one** of the following is an advantage to a business of having a centralised organisational structure?
Select **one** answer. (1)

☐ A Decisions are made by people that may know their local customers better

☐ B Staff are able to have more input into the decision-making process

☐ C Consistent decisions will be made for the whole organisation

☐ D Branch managers may have increased motivation

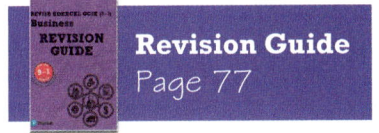

LEARN IT!

Remember, a centralised organisational structure is one in which most decisions are made at head office.

Hint

With multiple-choice questions, always aim to immediately rule out the options you know are incorrect.

(b) Which **one** of the following involves allowing potential customers to use a product before purchase?
Select **one** answer. (1)

☐ A Advertising
☐ B Branding
☐ C Special offers
☐ D Product trial

Revision Guide Page 63

Hint

Businesses use promotion techniques to create customer awareness of, interest in and desire for their products.

Set 3 Paper 2

Revision Guide Page 51

Hint

Selling assets is an **internal** source of finance, so you could explain why generating funds from within the business is better than using an external source of finance such as a bank loan.

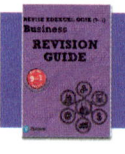

Revision Guide Page 71

Hint

Remember: with quality control there is a specialist employed to check the quality of products against agreed standards at the end of the production line. With quality assurance, every employee checks their own quality throughout.

Hint

Make sure your answer focuses on 'quality control' as opposed to just 'improving quality'.

(c) Explain **one** benefit to a business of raising finance by selling assets. (3)

....
....
....
....
....
....
....
....

(d) Explain **one** benefit to a business of having a quality control system in place. (3)

....
....
....
....
....
....
....
....

(Total for Question 1 = 8 marks)

2 (a) Which **two** of the following are examples of goods?
Select **two** answers. (2)

- [ ] **A** Hairdressers
- [ ] **B** Dentists
- [ ] **C** Shoes
- [ ] **D** Fridge freezer
- [ ] **E** Travel agent

(b) Which **two** of the following are advantages to a business of internal recruitment?
Select **two** answers. (2)

- [ ] **A** It is likely to result in a wider range of candidates
- [ ] **B** There may be a greater variety of fresh ideas
- [ ] **C** Candidates will always have the skills needed so no training will be required
- [ ] **D** It is likely to be quicker and cheaper
- [ ] **E** The firm will already be aware of its employees' skills, experiences and attitudes to work

Table 1 contains information about a new piece of equipment that a business will keep and use for four years.

Total profit over four years	£440 000
Cost of equipment	£550 000

Table 1

(c) Using the information in Table 1, calculate the average rate of return of the new equipment. You are advised to show your workings. (2)

.... %

Set 3 Paper 2

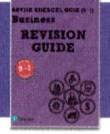

Revision Guide Page 60

Hint

Businesses can increase the life of a product using extension strategies. This involves slightly changing the product so that it has a fresh appeal to the target market or appeals to a new market segment.

Hint

This 'Explain' question is asking for a 'method' not a 'benefit'. Therefore, you need to explain a process as to how the life cycle of a product could be extended.

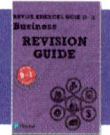

(d) Explain **one** method a business may use to extend the cycle of a product it sells. (3)

....
....
....
....
....
....
....
....

Revision Guide Page 77

Hint

A decentralised organisational structure allows managers to make decisions at a local level rather than decisions being made by those working at a head office.

(e) Explain **one** benefit to a business of having a decentralised organisational structure. (3)

....
....
....
....
....
....
....
....

(Total for Question 2 = 12 marks)

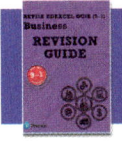

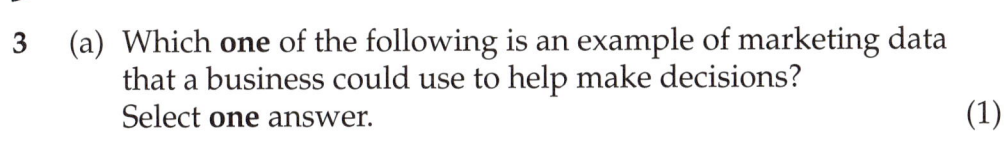

3 (a) Which **one** of the following is an example of marketing data that a business could use to help make decisions?
Select **one** answer. (1)

☐ **A** Customer opinion of a product

☐ **B** Financial accounts of a business

☐ **C** The interest rate that a bank would charge for loan capital

☐ **D** The number of competitors in a market

Figure 1 shows the sales revenue of three businesses that make up the entire market.

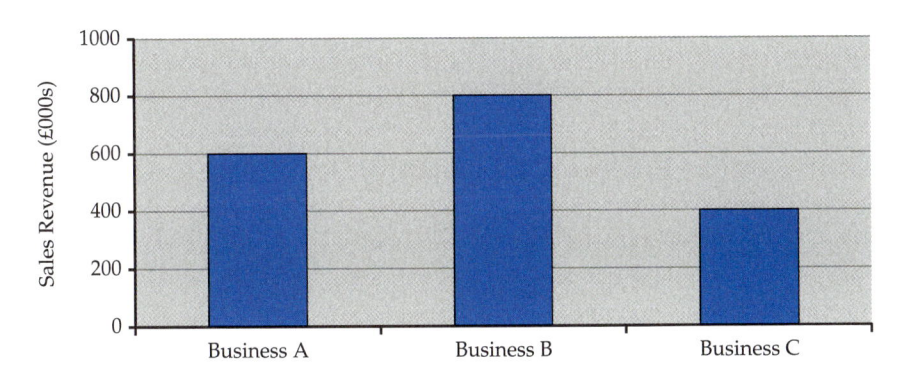

Figure 1

(b) Using the information in Figure 1, calculate the revenue of Business A as a percentage of the total market revenue. Show your answer to two decimal places. (2)

.... %

Set 3 Paper 2

Revision Guide Page 63

Hint

Special offers can include 'buy one get one free', free prize draws and selling at discounted rates. In using these, a business hopes to attract customers to purchase its products – but why could they have a negative effect on a business?

Revision Guide Page 85

LEARN IT!

Job enrichment can include giving employees more tasks to do, jobs that carry a greater degree of responsibility and opportunities to lead and make key decisions.

Watch out!

Read the question carefully. Make sure you give a benefit to the business and not employees.

(c) Explain **one** drawback to a business of using special offers to promote a product. (3)

....
....
....
....
....
....
....
....

(d) Explain **one** benefit to a business of implementing a job enrichment programme for its employees. (3)

....
....
....
....
....
....
....
....

(e) Discuss the drawback of insufficient communication to a business. (6)

....

....

....

....

....

....

....

....

....

....

....

....

....

....

(Total for Question 3 = 15 marks)

TOTAL FOR SECTION A = 35 MARKS

Set 3 Paper 2

Revision Guide Page 78

Watch out!

This question asks you to 'Discuss the drawback', so make sure you only write about the negative impact on the business.

Hint

Remember to use connectives, such as 'therefore', 'this leads to' and 'as a result', to show the links you make.

Approaching the question

You could answer this question in one of the following two ways.

- Give two separate drawbacks in two clear paragraphs, which together contain a total of five linked strands of development.
- Provide one drawback in one paragraph, with a total of five linked strands of development arising from the point you make.

SECTION B
Answer ALL questions
Read the following extract carefully and then answer Questions 4, 5 and 6.
Write your answers in the spaces provided.

IKEA is a Swedish-founded multinational retailer that designs and sells ready-to-assemble furniture, kitchen appliances and home accessories. Until now *IKEA* stores have been huge out-of-town warehouses where customers walk round a large showroom before collecting their furniture from a 'market hall' warehouse at the end. However, this format is changing.

IKEA has recently opened a new city centre shop on Tottenham Court Road, London. The shop is the retailer's revised strategy in the UK to bring *IKEA* to the heart of urban areas as it tries to respond to the demand from the continued growth of people living in cities. An IKEA spokesperson, *IKEA* UK and Ireland Country Manager, said that, *'Urbanisation and inner-city living are trends that continue to dominate the market. By launching this new approach and investing in our online offer and services, we are working to ensure IKEA remains affordable, convenient and sustainable, both now and in the future.'*

The new Tottenham Court Road shop will specialise in kitchens and wardrobes, giving customers the advice and inspiration they need to browse, plan and order their furniture. *IKEA* will offer its customers a bespoke service, using interactive software to help them design their dream rooms at affordable prices.

IKEA has been investing heavily in online, logistics and distribution in a move to cut its home delivery times from one to two weeks to three to four days. An IKEA spokesperson said that this investment was not a reaction to *Amazon* or any particular retailer but a response to changing customer demands.

IKEA takes pride in how it treats staff members, as it believes that they are the heart of the brand. The retailer invests heavily in its staff, providing many opportunities for job rotation and job enrichment. In 2018, 1 711 workers took a new job opportunity within the business and 523 employees were promoted internally. *IKEA* hopes that this investment in staff and its new strategy of opening inner-city stores will help the business to continue to grow over the coming years.

(Source adapted from: https://www.ikea.com/gb/en/this-is-ikea/newsroom/press-release/ikea-to-open-new-shop-on-londons-tottenham-court-road-as-part-of-new-city-centre-approach/ *and* https://www.ikea.com/gb/en/doc/content-snippet-links/ikea-ikea-uk-annual-summary-financial-year-2018__1364661808789.pdf)

Set 3 Paper 2

4 (a) Outline **one** benefit to *IKEA* of creating a person specification as part of the process of recruiting sales assistants for its new inner-city stores. (2)

....
....
....
....
....

The new inner-city *IKEA* stores will not hold any stock due to the limited amount of space available.

(b) Analyse the impact to *IKEA* of using just-in-time stock control in its new inner-city stores. (6)

....
....
....
....
....
....
....
....
....
....
....
....
....
....

(Total for Question 4 = 8 marks)

Approaching the question

You can answer 'Analyse' questions in one of the following two of ways.
- Make one point then develop it using five linked strands.
- Make two points in two separate paragraphs, ensuring there is a total of five linked strands of development across the two points.

Revision Guide Page 81

Watch out!

To demonstrate **Application** you need to use words related to the case study but not those in the question – so in this case, you would not gain any marks for writing 'IKEA' or 'new inner-city stores'.

Revision Guide Page 69

LEARN IT!

Just-in-time (JIT) stock control is a stock management system where stock is delivered only when it is needed by the production system, so no stock is stored by a business.

Hint

This question asks you to 'Analyse the impact', so you can address either the benefits or the drawbacks for *IKEA* of using just-in-time stock control – as impacts can be either.

5   Figure 2 shows the total number of yearly website visits on *IKEA's* site between 2013 and 2018.

Website visits (billions): 1.35 (2013), 1.6 (2014), 1.9 (2015), 2.1 (2016), 2.3 (2017), 2.5 (2018)

Figure 2

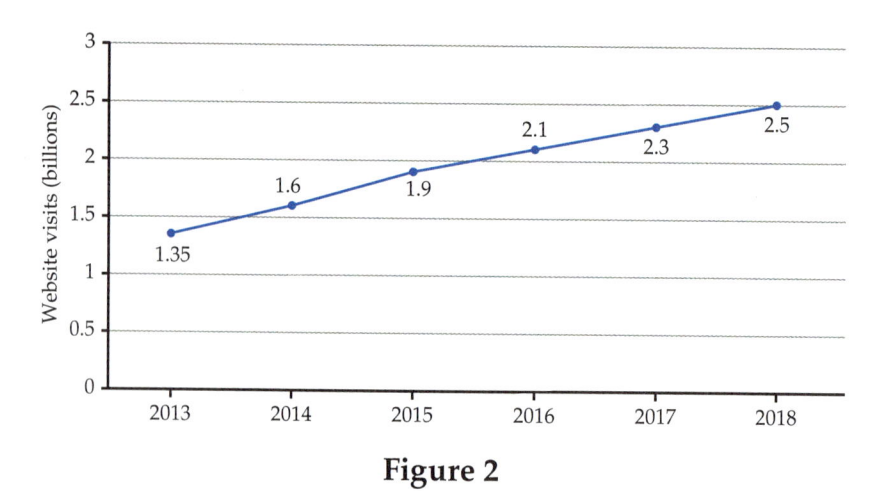

Table 2 contains some information regarding *IKEA's* revenue and net profit in 2017 and 2018.

	2018	**2017**
Revenue (€ bn)	38.8	38.3
Net profit (€ bn)	1.47	2.47

Table 2

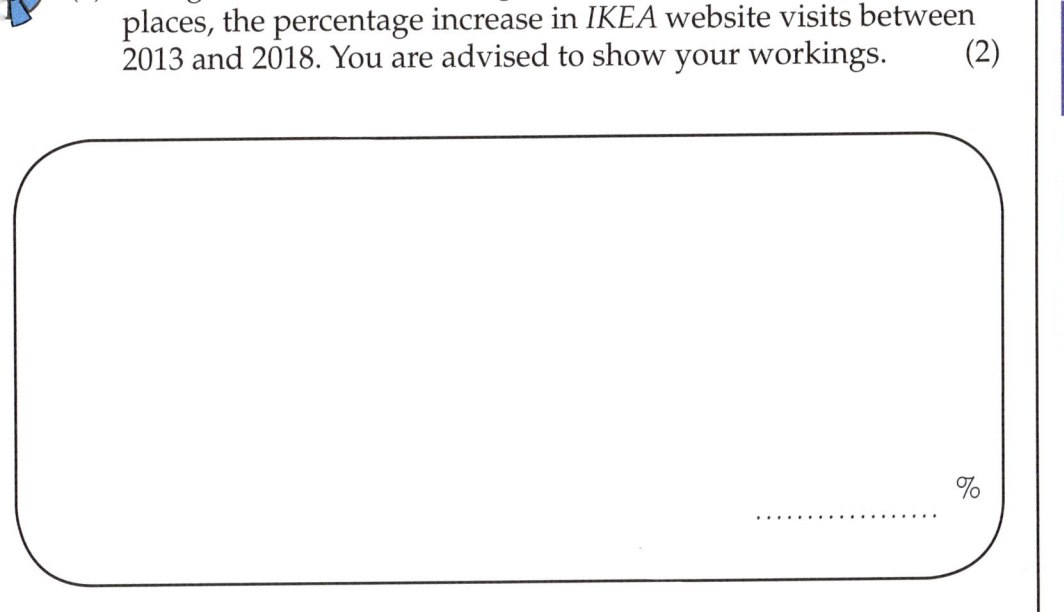

(a) Using the information in Figure 2, calculate, to two decimal places, the percentage increase in *IKEA* website visits between 2013 and 2018. You are advised to show your workings. (2)

.... %

(b) Using the information in Table 2, calculate, to two decimal places, *IKEA's* net profit margin in 2018. You are advised to show your workings. (2)

.... %

Set 3 Paper 2

Revision Guide Pages 84–85

(c) Analyse the benefit to *IKEA* of it investing 'heavily in its staff'.

(6)

....
....
....
....
....
....
....
....
....
....
....
....
....
....
....
....
....
....

(Total for Question 5 = 10 marks)

Hint

IKEA 'invests heavily in its staff' is a line from the case study – it means *IKEA* takes good care of its staff and spends money training and developing them. Make sure you read the case study carefully, as it contains the information you need to make your response specific to *IKEA*'s situation and to determine how *IKEA* does this and how it benefits them.

Watch out!

You must only talk about the **benefits to** *IKEA* – as this is what the question requires.

Approaching the question

You can either choose to give one benefit with five linked strands of development, or two separate benefits with five linked strands of development across the two points. Use connectives, such as 'this will lead to', 'therefore' and 'as a result', to show these links.

6 (a) State **one** drawback to *IKEA* from selling its products online. (1)

....

....

(b) Outline **one** benefit to *IKEA* from its use of technology in providing its service in the new inner-city stores. (2)

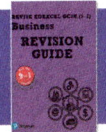

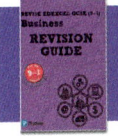

....

....

....

....

....

....

Set 3 Paper 2

Revision Guide Page 49

Hint

It is important to think carefully about how you conclude your response. It is a good idea to state the most significant reason why you have picked a particular option, and to mention what your decision might depend on. For instance, if you picked Option 2 (opening more inner-city stores), is there a scenario where investing in large out-of-town stores (Option 1) might be better?

To continue to see growth in sales, *IKEA* is considering two different options.

Option 1: Continue to invest in large out-of-town stores.

Option 2: Open more inner-city stores that provide a bespoke service.

(c) Justify which **one** of these two options *IKEA* should choose. (9)

....

....

....

....

....

....

....

....

....

....

....

....

....

....

....

....

....

....

....

....

....

....

....

(Total for Question 6 = 12 marks)

TOTAL FOR SECTION B = 30 MARKS

Approaching the question

'Justify' questions require you to give a balanced response. Many students make the mistake of discussing both options, but still end up giving a one-sided argument – for example, giving the positive of one option and the negative of another, or giving the benefits of both options. Both of these approaches would limit the marks you would be awarded for **Evaluation**.

The best approach is to pick an option and then discuss the benefit and drawback of that option in the context of the case study. This would form a balanced argument that gains you credit for Evaluation.

When answering a 'Justify' question, to gain marks for **Application** you must apply your knowledge to the context of the case study. To demonstrate this skill, make sure you use words and phrases from the case study – such as 'the Swedish furniture retailer', 'out-of-town warehouses', 'a bespoke service' and 'design dream rooms at affordable prices' – throughout your response, including in the conclusion.

SECTION C

Answer ALL questions.
Read the following extract carefully and then answer Question 7.
Write your answers in the spaces provided.

Jack's is a new cut-price brand of supermarket owned by *Tesco* and launched to rival *Aldi* and *Lidl*. The new concept is named after Jack Cohen, who founded *Tesco* 99 years ago. The new venture has been funded through internal finance provided by *Tesco*, with the company investing between £20 and £25 million. *Tesco* CEO, Dave Lewis, indicated that the new model would have a focus on low prices and an emphasis on quality British produce.

This strategy is in response to competition from *Aldi* and *Lidl*, who have increased their market share to 13.1 per cent over the past five years. The supermarket industry is changing and, as *Aldi's* and *Lidl's* success proves, customers are turning to cheaper shops.

Lewis hopes to open 15 more *Jack's* stores across the country within a year and to employ 250 new employees. The staff will be recruited externally and will earn a 'base rate' of £9 per hour, which is 58p more than a *Tesco* worker (as at November 2018). However, *Jack's* workers won't get a 10 per cent discount as *Tesco* staff do, and they will not enjoy any bonuses. As part of a strategy of keeping costs down, staff will be able to wear their own clothes, with only an apron and a name badge necessary.

Jack's will stock around 2 600 products of which 1 800 will be own-label items (a typical *Tesco* stocks more than 25 000 items). It will stock some household brands such as *Coca-Cola* but the focus is on *Jack's* own-label products.

Lewis stated that *Jack's* will use the company's existing supply base to keep costs down and that this, combined with more efficient, cheaper-to-run stores, will mean customers get a better deal.

(Source: https://inews.co.uk/news/consumer/everything-you-need-to-know-about-jacks-tesco/)

7 (a) Define the term external recruitment. (1)

....

....

Figure 3 shows the market share (of the total grocery market) of *Tesco*, *Aldi* and *Lidl* between 2014 and 2018.

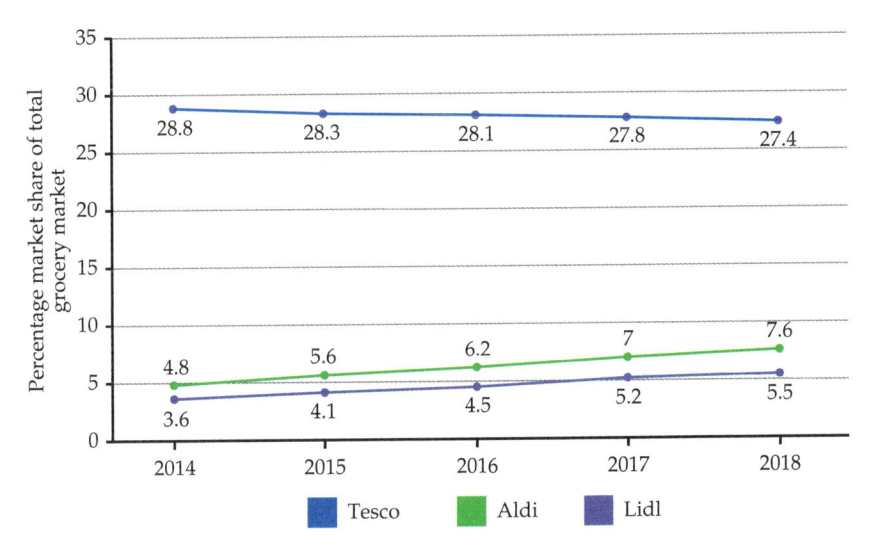

Year	Tesco	Aldi	Lidl
2014	28.8	4.8	3.6
2015	28.3	5.6	4.1
2016	28.1	6.2	4.5
2017	27.8	7.0	5.2
2018	27.4	7.6	5.5

Figure 3

(Source: https://www.statista.com/statistics/300656/grocery-market-share-in-great-britain-year-on-year-comparison/)

(b) Using Figure 3, identify which of the supermarkets saw a decrease in its market share between 2014 and 2018. (1)

....

....

Set 3 Paper 2

Table 3 shows some financial information relating to *Tesco* for 2017 and 2018.

	2017 (£ million)	2018 (£ million)
Revenue	55 917	57 491
Cost of sales	53 015	54 141
Other operating expenses	1 995	1 663

Table 3

(Source://www.tescoplc.com/media/474793/tesco_ar_2018.pdf)

(c) Using Table 3, calculate *Tesco's* gross profit for 2018. You are advised to show your workings. (2)

£ .... m

Revision Guide Page 73

LEARN IT!

Gross profit is the profit that a business makes on its trading activity before any indirect costs have been deducted.

The cost of sales is the cost of buying, producing and distributing products and services.

To calculate gross profit, subtract the cost of sales from the sales revenue (or turnover).

Watch out!

Sometimes you will be given more information than you need and you may have to work out which is relevant. For example, which data is **not** relevant to calculating gross profit for 2018 in Table 3?

To improve the productivity of staff and therefore the performance of the business, *Jack's* is considering two different methods of motivation.

Option 1: Increase the annual salary of workers.

Option 2: Pay workers a bonus based on the success of the store.

(d) Justify which **one** of these two options *Jack's* should choose. (9)

Set 3 Paper 2

Revision Guide Page 84

Hint

Application is one of the three skill areas assessed in the 9-mark 'Justify' questions. There is no numerical count of how many times you use context in your response (unlike for the skill of **Analysis**, which requires you to have a minimum of five linked strands of development to maximise your marks.). You need to aim to use the context thoroughly, throughout your answer. Not every single sentence needs to be applied, but you do need to use Application throughout your answer, including in your conclusion.

Watch out!

When answering 9-mark 'Justify' questions, many students forget to demonstrate the skill of **Application** in their conclusion.

Set 3 Paper 2

....
....
....
....

Approaching the question

Try taking a three-paragraph approach when answering the 9-mark 'Justify' questions.

- Paragraph 1 looks at the benefit of the chosen option.
- Paragraph 2 considers the drawback of the chosen option.
- Paragraph 3 provides a conclusion, which puts the benefit and drawback into context.

(e) Evaluate whether having lower prices than competitors is the best way for *Jack's* to compete in the grocery market. You should use the information provided as well as your knowledge of business. (12)

Watch out!

To show the skill of **Application** throughout your answer, make sure you do the following.

- Refer to the grocery market and to *Jack's* itself, as well as *Jack's* competitors *Aldi* and *Lidl*.
- Use phrases from the case study such as 'supermarkets', 'own-branded goods' and 'discount stores'.

Watch out!

To show the skill of **Analysis** throughout your answer you should do the following.

- Ensure your answer has a minimum of five linked strands of development. These can be spread across the two points you make.
- Use connectives, such as 'this means that', 'therefore' and 'this leads to', to demonstrate the links you make.

Set 3 Paper 2

....
....

(Total for Question 7 = 25 marks)
TOTAL FOR SECTION C = 25 MARKS
TOTAL FOR PAPER = 90 MARKS

Hint

A counter argument could include any other way of competing, such as advertising, building a strong brand, having a quality product, widening distribution channels and having a highly differentiated product. There are many you could use – but just pick the one argument you think is most relevant to *Jack's*.

Hint

Use the 'It depends' rule as a way of showing insight and sophistication in your conclusion. In this case, consider other factors that may affect whether having lower prices is the best way to compete.

Approaching the question

Try this approaching this question using a three-paragraph structure.
- Paragraph 1: Analyse why having lower prices is the best way for *Jack's* to compete in the grocery market.
- Paragraph 2: Address why having lower prices is not the best way of competing. One way of doing this is to suggest an alternative method of competing and analyse why it is better. For instance, *Jack's* could focus on quality instead, or promotion in order to gain better recognition in the market.
- Paragraph 3: Make the final paragraph your conclusion. Which side of the argument is stronger and why? What additional factors might your decision depend on? Make sure you use the case study to argue your point of view from *Jack's* perspective.

Set 1 Paper 1 Answers

The answers to the longer questions are sample answers – there are many ways you could answer these questions.

SECTION A
Answer ALL questions.
Write your answers in the spaces provided.
Some questions must be answered with a cross in a box ☒.
If you change your mind about an answer, put a line through the box ▧ and then mark your new answer with a cross ☒.

1 (a) Which **one** of the following is an example of a variable cost? Select **one** answer. (1)

☐ A Rent
☒ B Wages ✓
☐ C Loan repayments
☐ D Buildings insurance

(b) Which **one** of the following is an example of a customer need? Select **one** answer. (1)

☐ A Differentiation
☐ B Profit
☒ C Convenience ✓
☐ D Customer feedback

(c) Explain **one** reason why a business would carry out market research. (3)

A business would carry out market research in order to find out the opinions and needs of customers. ✓ Therefore, they have a better chance of developing products and services to satisfy customer needs, ✓ leading to greater sales revenue. ✓

(d) Explain **one** benefit to a business of increasing its range of products. (3)

If a business increases its range of products it will be able to target a wider range of customers. ✓ This will lead to more sources of revenue. ✓ Therefore, there is less risk of the business failing if one product line loses popularity. ✓

(Total for Question 1 = 8 marks)

2 (a) Which **two** of the following are features of a business plan? Select **two** answers. (2)

☐ A Job description
☐ B Social media posts
☒ C Cash-flow forecast ✓
☒ D Business aims and objectives ✓
☐ E Employment legislation

(b) Which **two** of the following describe the purpose of business activity? Select **two** answers. (2)

☐ A To take risks
☒ B To meet customer needs ✓
☐ C To carry out market research
☒ D To produce goods and services ✓
☐ E To make decisions about how resources are used

Figure 1 contains information about a small business for one month's trading.
The business has estimated that it needs to sell 180 units per month in order to break even.

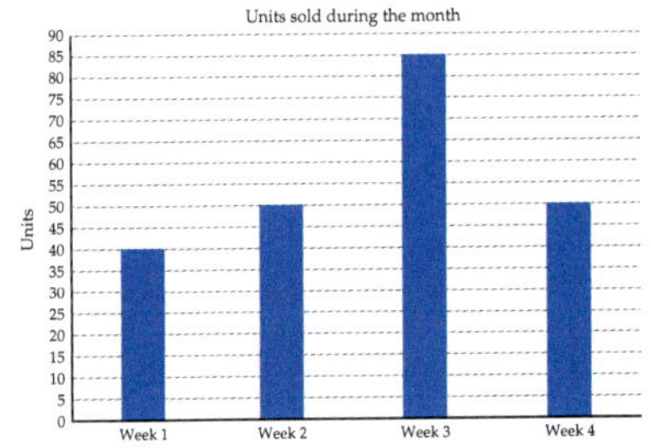

Units sold during the month

Week 1: 40
Week 2: 50
Week 3: 85
Week 4: 50

Figure 1

(c) Using the information in Figure 1, calculate the margin of safety for the business. You are advised to show your workings. (2)

Total monthly sales = sum of all units sold in the month
= 40 +
50 +
85 +
50
225 units

Break-even point = 180 units

Margin of safety = expected sales − break-even point
= 225 − 180 = ✓

..........45..........✓ units

(d) Explain **one** reason that a business owner might use a market map. (3)

A business owner might use a market map to identify a gap in a market. ✓ This would help the owner identify an opportunity where customer needs were not currently being met. ✓ As a result, the business would have a greater chance of success by targeting these market needs, as there is less competition. ✓

(e) Explain **one** disadvantage to a business of an increase in interest rates. (3)

The disadvantage to a business of rising interest rates is that demand for its products or services might fall. ✓ This is because its customers will have less disposable income ✓ and will therefore spend less on certain types of products. ✓

(Total for Question 2 = 12 marks)

3 (a) Which **one** of the following is a feature of a franchise? Select **one** answer. (1)

☐ A The franchisee keeps all profits
☐ B The business has unlimited liability
☐ C The franchisee can sell shares in the business
☒ D The business has limited liability ✓

Table 1 gives the cash-flow forecast for a small business.

	Jan (£)	Feb (£)	Mar (£)
Cash inflow	8 500	20 200	8 200
Cash outflow	5 500	7 300 ✓	5 500
Net cash-flow	3 000	12 900	2 700
Opening balance	−2 000	1 000	13 900
Closing balance	1 000 ✓	13 900	16 600

Table 1

(b) Complete Table 1 by calculating the missing values. You are advised to show your workings. (2)

Opening balance for Feb = £1000 = Closing balance for Jan

Net cash-flow = Cash inflow − Cash outflow

So, cash outflow = Cash inflow − Net cash-flow = £20 200 − £12 900
£7 300

(c) Explain **one** way a business can use the marketing mix to improve competitiveness. (3)

A business could improve competitiveness by lowering its prices. ✓ If it can reduce its variable costs on a product, it can reduce prices without reducing the profit margin. ✓ More people will want to buy it at the reduced cost, so demand will increase. ✓

(d) Explain **one** disadvantage of setting up a business in a location close to its competitors. (3)

There will be more competition. ✓ Therefore the business may need to lower its prices to compete. ✓ This may result in a lower profit margin on each item sold. ✓

Set 1 Paper 1 Answers

(e) Discuss how stakeholders can affect business decisions. (6)

Employees can affect business decisions by putting pressure on managers to improve working conditions and pay. In order to keep workers happy and retain the best employees, a business should think carefully before making any decision that could reduce employee incomes. As a result, a business might need to make a choice between lowering costs and retaining a motivated workforce. If a decision is made without considering employees' interests, it could lead to employees choosing to leave the company to work for a competitor. Another stakeholder group that could affect business decisions is customers. Because customer tastes and preferences change, a business will have to adapt its products and services to meet those tastes and preferences. This will influence how a business invests in new product development, such as encouraging a business to conduct market research to determine what customers want and whether there is a need for a different product offering.

(Total for Question 3 = 15 marks)
TOTAL FOR SECTION A = 35 MARKS

Writing a good answer

'Discuss' questions will ask you to look at a likely impact, benefit, drawback or similar. In a 'Discuss' question you should:
- show your **Knowledge and Understanding (AO1)** by giving one or two clear points
- include a minimum of five linked development points across the 1–2 points you have made, to demonstrate your **Analysis (AO3a)**.

A very strong answer because...

✓ **Understanding**: This answer considers two different stakeholder groups (employees and customers), developing the reasons for how each affects business decisions. It shows understanding of motivation, customer needs and market research.

✓ **Analysis**: There are six linked strands of development, which more than covers the requirement for a minimum of five, with excellent use of connectives – such as 'because' and 'as a result'.

SECTION B
Answer ALL questions.
Read the following extract carefully and then answer Questions 4, 5 and 6.
Write your answers in the spaces provided.

Sid is the owner of *Bluecoat Builders Ltd*, a small building company that specialises in loft conversions. Sid started the company 12 years ago and now employs four full-time builders. In that time, *Bluecoat Builders* has developed a reputation for excellent customer service. Most of Sid's new customers now come through recommendations from customers' friends and family.

Bluecoat Builders' trade is seasonal, with the majority of work coming in the summer months when it is more convenient to carry out work on roofs. To boost sales in the winter months, Sid has introduced a special offer of free decoration (paint or wallpaper) with all loft conversions from December to February.

For each job, Sid has to hire scaffolding from a local company, which can be very expensive. In the long-term, Sid has decided it would be cheaper to buy the scaffolding so that the company owns it as an asset. The scaffolding will cost £3500.

As a building company, *Bluecoat Builders* has to comply with UK Building Regulations 2010. For example, every loft conversion the company completes must receive an energy performance certificate following an inspection by the local council.

Free decoration on loft conversions during December and January!

Grow your home this winter with a
LOFT CONVERSION

With 12 years of expertise in loft conversions, *Bluecoat Builders* can help you create your dream home!
Call Sid on 01845 567890 today!

Labour only. Paint or wallpaper to be supplied by client.

---

4 (a) Outline **one** benefit to *Bluecoat Builders* of having a reputation for excellent customer service. (2)

This will lead to more customers recommending their loft conversions to friends and family,✓ which will lead to more customers requesting a quote for building work from Sid.✓

(b) Analyse the impact on *Bluecoat Builders* of UK building regulations legislation. (6)

UK building regulations may mean that each project takes longer for Bluecoat Builders to complete. For example, if the local council has to inspect each loft conversion, this will mean each loft conversion can be delayed due to Sid having to wait for the inspector to complete their work. As a result, Bluecoat Builders might complete fewer projects each year, therefore its margin of safety could fall leading to a higher risk that the business will not break even.
By meeting its legal requirements, Bluecoat Builders could be more likely to produce loft conversions of a higher quality and building work that is safer for customers. As a result, the company is more likely to receive good publicity and reinforce its reputation for excellent customer service in the building trade. This will ensure more customers for Bluecoat Builders and increased profits, so expanding the business.

(Total for Question 4 = 8 marks)

Writing a good answer

In an 'Analyse' question you should:
- clearly **apply your answer to the context** throughout (AO2)
- give one or two clear points and a minimum of five linked development points, to demonstrate your **Analysis (AO3a)**.

A very strong answer because...

✓ **Application**: The answer uses the context through reference to loft conversions, the council, local inspectors and the firm's customer service.

✓ **Analysis**: The answer identifies two impacts – negative (projects take longer) and positive (higher quality). Both are well developed by three linked strands.

---

5 One impact of legislation on businesses is that it results in additional costs being incurred.
Sid has drawn up the following financial information.

Annual fixed costs	£150 000
Average cost per loft conversion	£11 000
Average price customers pay for a loft conversion	£38 000

Table 1

(a) Using the information in Table 1, calculate to the nearest whole number, the number of loft conversions *Bluecoat Builders* would need to install each year in order to break even. You are advised to show your workings. (2)

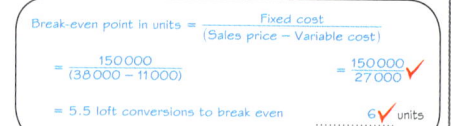

$$\text{Break-even point in units} = \frac{\text{Fixed cost}}{(\text{Sales price} - \text{Variable cost})}$$

$$= \frac{150\,000}{(38\,000 - 11\,000)} = \frac{150\,000}{27\,000} ✓$$

= 5.5 loft conversions to break even   6 ✓ units

Sid has learned that the cost for the council building inspector to review the work of all local builders is to increase by 17 per cent. On *Bluecoat Builders'* last project, the building inspection cost £250.

(b) Calculate, to two decimal places, how much more *Bluecoat Builders* will have to pay for its work to be inspected after the increase in cost. You are advised to show your workings. (2)

New cost = Original cost × percentage increase
= £250.00 × 0.17 ✓
= £42.50
£42.50 ✓

(c) Analyse the impact on *Bluecoat Builders* of its business being seasonal. (6)

One impact of the seasonality of Bluecoat Builders is that the company might have cash-flow problems in the winter months, when demand for building work is low. If cash outflows are lower than cash inflows, then the business will have a negative cash-flow and this could result in insolvency. This could lead to Sid failing to pay his four full-time employees.
Another impact of seasonality is that Sid might need to offer discounts to his customers, in order to boost demand in the winter. He has already done this by offering free decoration between December and February on all loft conversions. One consequence of these special offers, however, is Sid's profit margin will be lower on each project; therefore, it will take Bluecoat Builders longer to reach break-even. Without generating enough overall profit, Sid may find it difficult to grow his business with retained profit.

(Total for Question 5 = 10 marks)

Writing a good answer

'Analyse' questions will ask you to look at an impact, advantage, drawback or similar.
In an 'Analyse' question you should:
- clearly **apply your answer to the context** throughout your answer (AO2)
- give one or two clear points and a minimum of five linked development points, to demonstrate your **Analysis (AO3a)**.

A very strong answer because...

✓ **Application**: There are various references in both paragraphs to the building trade of which *Bluecoat Builders* is a part; for example, 'building work', 'loft conversions', 'four full-time employees' and 'free decoration between December and February'.

✓ **Analysis**: This answer demonstrates the two-paragraph approach, with at least five linked development points across both paragraphs. There is also good use of connectives, such as 'If... then...', 'Another impact of...' and 'One consequence of...', to make these links.

---

6 (a) State **one** objective Sid might set for his business. (1)

To achieve a certain amount of sales revenue from loft conversions during the next year.✓

(b) Outline **one** benefit to Sid of running a private limited company. (2)

One benefit is that Sid will have limited liability.✓ As a result, he can only lose the value of his investment in the company, such as £3500 if he chooses to purchase the scaffolding using his own personal savings.✓

126

Set 1 Paper 1 Answers

Sid is considering two options for raising £3500 to purchase the scaffolding, so that the company owns it as an asset.

Option 1: Taking out a bank loan.
Option 2: Using retained profit.

(c) Justify which **one** of these two options *Bluecoat Builders* should choose. (9)

I think taking a bank loan is the best option. If Sid's application for a bank loan is successful, he could receive the money the next day. This would mean he could purchase the scaffolding straightaway and wouldn't need to rent the equipment on upcoming projects. As a result, Bluecoat Builders' variable costs per project would fall. The business might therefore have a stronger cash-flow if the loan repayments are lower than the cost of renting the scaffolding.

However, if Sid takes out a bank loan to purchase the scaffolding, he will be increasing his monthly fixed costs because he will have to make regular loan repayments. These loan repayments will incur interest charges. During periods of lower demand, such as in the winter, the building company might have a negative cash-flow leading to liquidity problems. Consequently, Sid might have to increase the price of each loft conversion to cover the additional fixed cost of the loan repayment.

Overall, I think a bank loan is a better option to finance the scaffolding than using retained profit. This is because Bluecoat Builders might not have £3500 retained profit spare to finance the scaffolding. However, this decision may depend on the rate of interest Sid is able to secure on any loan he takes out.

(Total for Question 6 = 12 marks)
TOTAL FOR SECTION B = 30 MARKS

Writing a good answer

'Justify' questions will ask you to make a choice between two options. **There is no need to discuss both options.**

When answering a 'Justify' question, aim to write three paragraphs.

- **Paragraph 1:** Select the option you feel is best and state why, using at least three linked strands of development to demonstrate **Analysis (AO3a)**. Make sure you refer to the context throughout, to demonstrate **Application (AO2)**.
- **Paragraph 2:** Explain a drawback of the option you have chosen, to show balance and **Evaluation (AO3b)**. Again, include at least three linked strands of development to demonstrate **Analysis (AO3a)**, and refer to context to demonstrate **Application (AO2)**. By including three linked strands of development in both paragraphs, you can be more confident that you are covering the overall requirement of five linked strands of development for this answer.
- **Paragraph 3:** Conclude by giving the main reason why you selected your option. Use the 'It depends' rule. This is another way of demonstrating **Evaluation (AO3b)**, and should also refer to the context for **Application (AO2)**.

A very strong answer because…

✓ **Application:** The case study is referred to in detail. For example, the first paragraph refers to 'upcoming projects' and the 'renting' of scaffolding; the second paragraph refers to increasing the price of 'loft conversions' and the lower demand in 'winter' months; the conclusion refers to the price of the scaffolding being '£350'.

✓ **Analysis:** There are more than five linked strands of development across the first two paragraphs; these are clearly identified by the effective use of connectives such as 'this would mean', 'as a result' and 'consequently'.

✓ **Evaluation:** This is a balanced argument that considers one advantage and one disadvantage of the bank loan. The conclusion is logical and clearly states the main reason why Option 1 has been chosen, successfully justifying why this option is better than the alternative. Further credit may be given for the effective use of the 'It depends' rule when stating that the choice may depend on the rate of interest applied to the loan.

SECTION C
Answer ALL questions.
Read the following extract carefully and then answer Question 7.
Write your answers in the spaces provided.

Spectrum Paints was established by Dafne Forbes in 2012. The company manufactures a unique range of paints for domestic customers. *Spectrum Paints* is a premium brand distributed through small independent home improvement retailers. As such, it is not a large company and its products are not as well known as other paint brands such as *Crown* or *Dulux*. Neither is its product offering stocked in major retailers such as B&Q.

The company's unique selling point is its 'Trio Range', a pack of three paints in a set of complementary colours to decorate a room.

As the company has grown, its current manufacturing facilities are no longer suitable and Dafne is looking for larger premises. Dafne would like the new premises to be big enough to include a showroom and shop, so that customers can buy direct from *Spectrum Paints*.

Spectrum Paints imports most of the materials that are used to make its emulsion paints. Many of the raw materials are manufactured using crude oil and so they are affected by global oil prices. Over the past three years oil prices have been rising and this has increased the company's costs. Dafne has explored a number of options to help boost revenue in light of these external influences.

---

7 (a) State **one** factor Dafne might consider when choosing a new location for *Spectrum Paints*. (1)

Cost of the rent/mortgage on a new decorating showroom and shop ✓

Figure 2 shows the price of Brent crude oil per barrel between 2014 and 2018.

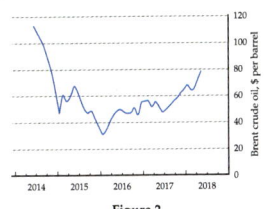

Figure 2

(b) Identify the years when Brent crude oil prices fell below $40 per barrel. (1)

2015 and 2016 ✓

(c) Outline **one** way that a fall in consumer incomes could affect *Spectrum Paints*. (2)

If consumer incomes fall then fewer people will be willing to spend money on redecorating their homes, especially not using premium paint, as it is not essential. ✓ As a result, demand for Spectrum Paint's paint home decorating range would fall. ✓

Dafne has identified two ways that could help *Spectrum Paints* increase its revenue.

Option 1: Launch a new range of paint.
Option 2: Increase its current prices by 5 per cent.

(d) Justify which **one** of these two options Dafne should choose. (9)

If Dafne chooses Option 2 – to increase prices by 5% – Spectrum Paints will increase its revenue because each sale will bring in more money per pot of paint. As well as increasing revenue, this will also increase the profit margin (if variable costs don't rise). As Spectrum Paints is a premium brand, customers might not be put off by the price rise because the paint they are buying is a unique range, such as Spectrum's trio set. Furthermore, a 5% price rise is not that much for a premium product, as customers will expect to pay a premium price for a luxury paint brand.

However, a 5% rise will increase revenue per tin of paint, but it will do little to increase demand because it doesn't make the paint more desirable, unlike offering a trio pack. As a result, Spectrum Paints' rivals could improve their competitiveness by developing their paints or providing better customer service. If Spectrum Paints' market share goes to other manufacturers, this would mean that its revenue would actually fall.

In conclusion, increasing the price of paint is a better option than launching a new range of paints in order to increase revenue. Investing in a new line of paints would require considerable financial investment in new product development, and Spectrum Paints is unlikely to be able to finance this alongside moving to larger premises and opening a retail outlet. However, simply raising its current prices by 5% will not improve Spectrum Paints' competitiveness in the home decoration market, in the way that developing its range of paints might do. It also depends on other factors, for example, if Spectrum Paint's variable costs continue to go up due to rising oil prices, the 5% rise in revenue will have little impact on the company's profit margins.

Writing a good answer

'Justify' questions will ask you to make a choice between two options. **There is no need to discuss both options.**

When answering a 'Justify' question, aim to write three paragraphs.

- **Paragraph 1:** Select the option you feel is best and state why, using at least three linked strands of development to demonstrate **Analysis (AO3a)**. Make sure you refer to the context throughout, to demonstrate **Application (AO2)**.
- **Paragraph 2:** Explain a drawback of the option you have chosen, to show balance and **Evaluation (AO3b)**. Again, include at least three linked strands of development to demonstrate **Analysis (AO3a)**, and refer to context to demonstrate **Application (AO2)**. By including three linked strands of development in both paragraphs, you will be more confident that you are covering the overall requirement of five linked strands of development for this answer.
- **Paragraph 3:** Conclude by giving the main reason why you selected your option. Use the 'It depends' rule. This is another way of demonstrating **Evaluation (AO3b)**, and should also refer to the context for **Application (AO2)**.

A very strong answer because…

✓ **Application:** The case study is referred to in detail. The first paragraph refers to the information provided about types of paint and the premium brand, and the second paragraph makes repeated references to paint and the trio pack. The conclusion is also rooted in the case study through the link to rising oil prices.

✓ **Analysis:** Across the first two paragraphs there are six linked strands of development, clearly identified through the effective use of connectives such as 'as a result', 'furthermore' and 'however'. This more than covers the required minimum of five linked development points to maximise marks for Analysis.

✓ **Evaluation:** This is a balanced argument that considers one advantage and one disadvantage of increasing prices by 5 per cent. The conclusion is logical and clearly states the main reason why Option 2 has been chosen over Option 1. Further credit may be given for the effective use of the 'It depends' rule.

127

Set 1 Paper 1 Answers

The value of the pound has increased in recent months.

(e) Evaluate whether the value of the pound will help *Spectrum Paints* become more competitive in its market. You should use the information provided as well as your knowledge of business. (12)

A rise in the value of the pound will help Spectrum Paints lower its variable costs of producing paint. This is because some of its raw materials are bought from international markets. The rise in the value of the pound will benefit importers, as each pound will buy more of a foreign currency. As a result, the cost of raw materials such as oil-based chemicals and colour pigments will be lower. This means that Spectrum Paints could pass on this saving to customers by lowering the price of its paint, making its paint more desirable and competitive compared to other paint such as Dulux or Crown.

There are however other factors that could contribute to the competitiveness of Spectrum Paints, such as how well it markets and promotes its products. Spectrum Paints is not a large company and its products will not be as well known as other brands such as Crown or Dulux. Nor is it stocked in major retailers such as B&Q. In order to succeed, Spectrum Paints will have to spend more on promotion, which could then lead to its paint being stocked in a wider range of DIY and decorating outlets. This will further increase the awareness of the brand among consumers. As a result of stronger brand awareness, sales revenue will be likely to rise. However, this could contradict Dafne's strategy of selling through small independent retailers and opening her own retail outlet alongside the factory.

In conclusion, a rise in the value of the pound will help Spectrum Paints, but this might only be a short-term impact. Exchange rates fluctuate, and in the near future the value of the pound could fall, resulting in rising variable costs for the company, such as the varying price of oil between 2014 and 2018. Furthermore, the benefit experienced by a rise in the value of the pound is relative, because other paint manufacturers that import raw materials will also benefit from it, so Spectrum Paints would not gain any competitive advantage from this. Variable costs are important to competitiveness, but other factors such as the marketing mix are likely to be more important and sustainable in helping Spectrum Paints become a competitive business.

(Total for Question 7 = 25 marks)
TOTAL FOR SECTION C = 25 MARKS
TOTAL FOR PAPER = 90 MARKS

Writing a good answer

In an 'Evaluate' question you should aim for three paragraphs.

- Paragraph 1: Show your **Knowledge and Understanding (AO1)**; for example, give a definition of one of the key terms and use Business terms throughout. Then provide arguments in support of the statement, with at least three linked development points to show thorough **Analysis (AO3a)**. Use the context (AO2).
- Paragraph 2: Give alternative arguments, with at least three linked development points to show thorough **Analysis (AO3a)**. Use the context (AO2).

By including three linked strands of development in both paragraphs, you will be more confident that you are covering the overall requirement of five linked strands of development.

- Paragraph 3: Give a balanced conclusion to demonstrate your **Evaluation (AO3b)**, using the context and making use of the 'It depends' argument.

A very strong answer because...

✓ **Understanding**: The response demonstrates a sound understanding of exchange rates and the value of promotion for *Spectrum Paints*.

✓ **Application**: Excellent reference is made to the case study, for example paint-related materials and *Spectrum Paints*' competitors.

✓ **Analysis**: There are more than the five linked strands of development across the points made in the first two paragraphs. There is effective use of connectives to show these links.

✓ **Evaluation**: There is a balanced argument setting out the case for why both the value of the pound and promotion are important to competitiveness. It notes how the value of a currency will fluctuate, and that other UK manufacturers may also benefit from a rise in the value of the pound, so limiting the relative advantage to *Spectrum Paints*.

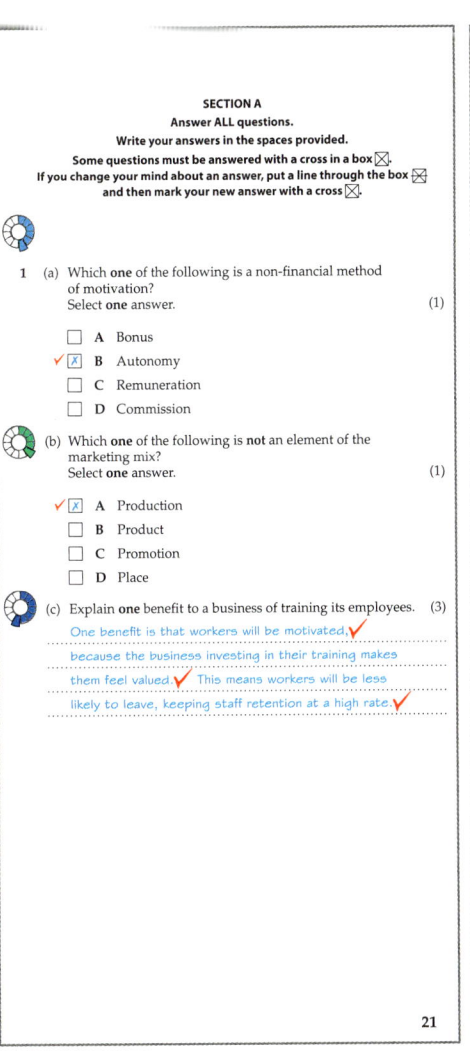

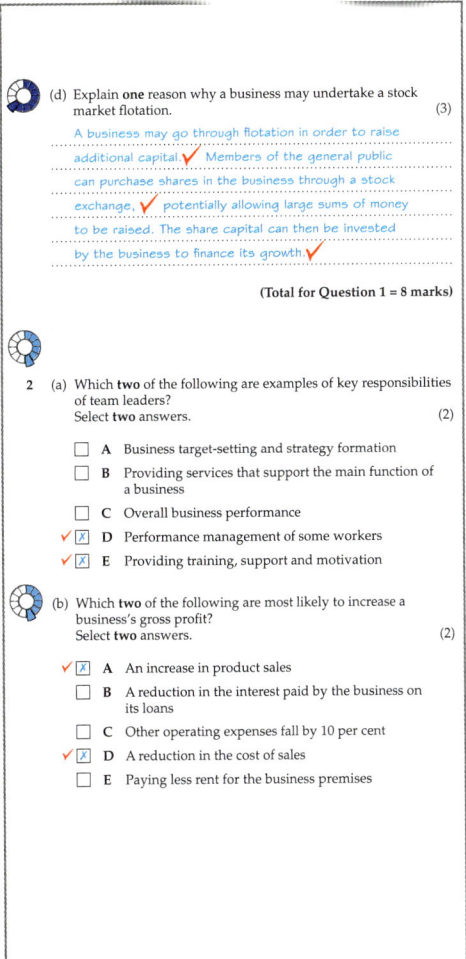

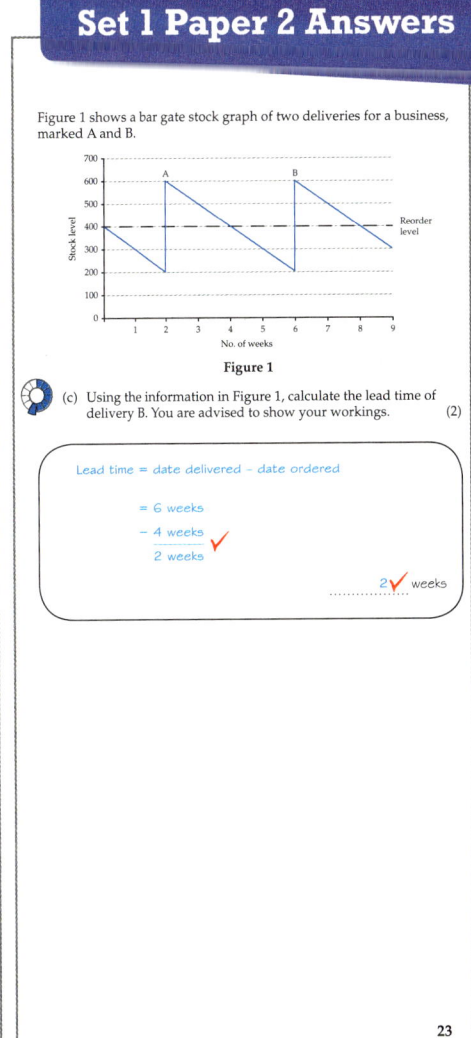

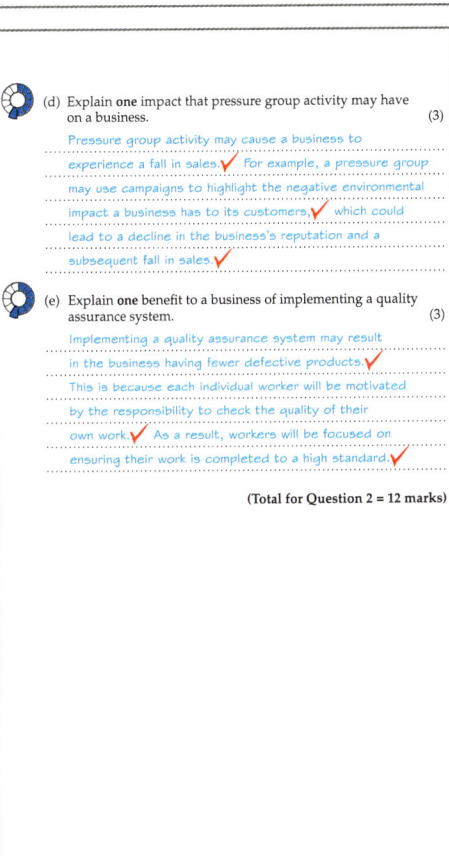

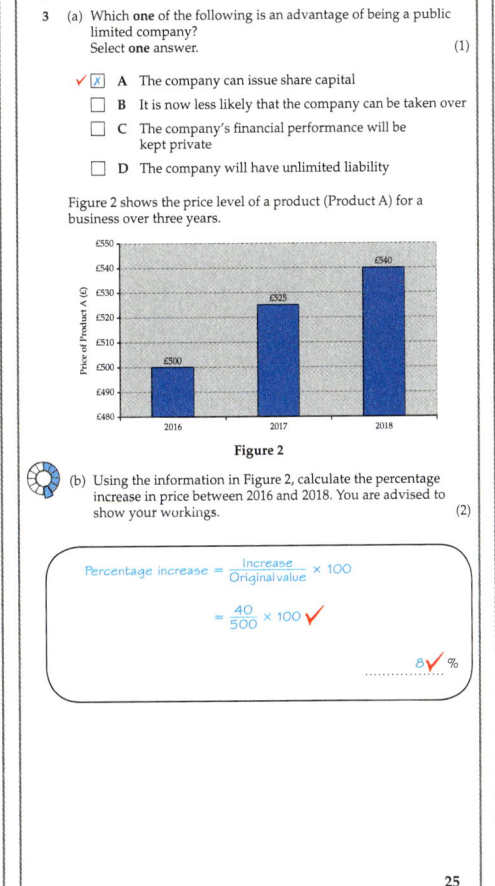

Set 1 Paper 2 Answers

SECTION A
Answer ALL questions.
Write your answers in the spaces provided.
Some questions must be answered with a cross in a box ☒.
If you change your mind about an answer, put a line through the box ☒ and then mark your new answer with a cross ☒.

1 (a) Which **one** of the following is a non-financial method of motivation?
   Select **one** answer. (1)
   ☐ A Bonus
   ✓ ☒ B Autonomy
   ☐ C Remuneration
   ☐ D Commission

(b) Which **one** of the following is **not** an element of the marketing mix?
   Select **one** answer. (1)
   ✓ ☒ A Production
   ☐ B Product
   ☐ C Promotion
   ☐ D Place

(c) Explain **one** benefit to a business of training its employees. (3)
   One benefit is that workers will be motivated,✓ because the business investing in their training makes them feel valued.✓ This means workers will be less likely to leave, keeping staff retention at a high rate.✓

(d) Explain **one** impact that pressure group activity may have on a business. (3)
   Pressure group activity may cause a business to experience a fall in sales.✓ For example, a pressure group may use campaigns to highlight the negative environmental impact a business has to its customers,✓ which could lead to a decline in the business's reputation and a subsequent fall in sales.✓

(e) Explain **one** benefit to a business of implementing a quality assurance system. (3)
   Implementing a quality assurance system may result in the business having fewer defective products.✓ This is because each individual worker will be motivated by the responsibility to check the quality of their own work.✓ As a result, workers will be focused on ensuring their work is completed to a high standard.✓

(Total for Question 2 = 12 marks)

(d) Explain **one** reason why a business may undertake a stock market flotation. (3)
   A business may go through flotation in order to raise additional capital.✓ Members of the general public can purchase shares in the business through a stock exchange,✓ potentially allowing large sums of money to be raised. The share capital can then be invested by the business to finance its growth.✓

(Total for Question 1 = 8 marks)

2 (a) Which **two** of the following are examples of key responsibilities of team leaders?
   Select **two** answers. (2)
   ☐ A Business target-setting and strategy formation
   ☐ B Providing services that support the main function of a business
   ☐ C Overall business performance
   ✓ ☒ D Performance management of some workers
   ✓ ☒ E Providing training, support and motivation

(b) Which **two** of the following are most likely to increase a business's gross profit?
   Select **two** answers. (2)
   ✓ ☒ A An increase in product sales
   ☐ B A reduction in the interest paid by the business on its loans
   ☐ C Other operating expenses fall by 10 per cent
   ✓ ☒ D A reduction in the cost of sales
   ☐ E Paying less rent for the business premises

3 (a) Which **one** of the following is an advantage of being a public limited company?
   Select **one** answer. (1)
   ✓ ☒ A The company can issue share capital
   ☐ B It is now less likely that the company can be taken over
   ☐ C The company's financial performance will be kept private
   ☐ D The company will have unlimited liability

Figure 2 shows the price level of a product (Product A) for a business over three years.

Figure 2

(b) Using the information in Figure 2, calculate the percentage increase in price between 2016 and 2018. You are advised to show your workings. (2)

$$\text{Percentage increase} = \frac{\text{Increase}}{\text{Original value}} \times 100$$

$$= \frac{40}{500} \times 100 \checkmark$$

........8✓........ %

Figure 1 shows a bar gate stock graph of two deliveries for a business, marked A and B.

Figure 1

(c) Using the information in Figure 1, calculate the lead time of delivery B. You are advised to show your workings. (2)

Lead time = date delivered − date ordered
= 6 weeks
− 4 weeks
2 weeks ✓

........2✓........ weeks

(c) Explain **one** way a business might use financial data to help make a decision. (3)
   A business could look at past sales data in order to find out seasonal variations in sales.✓ This would allow the business to order the correct amount of stock when it is needed,✓ therefore it won't be left with large amounts of unsold stock, which could lead to cash-flow problems.✓

(d) Explain **one** drawback to a business of recruiting employees externally. (3)
   A business could look at past sales data✓, therefore they would be able to find out if there were seasonal variations in their sales✓, this would then allow the business to ensure it orders the correct amount of stock for the time of year.✓

129

Set 1 Paper 2 Answers

(e) Discuss the benefit to a business of having a differentiated product. (6)

One benefit is that it makes a business's product stand out from the competition. This provides customers with a reason to purchase the product, which will improve the brand image of the business. This may lead to the business experiencing an increase in market share, giving the business a competitive edge over its rivals.

By differentiating the product, a business can add value. This means that a business is able to increase the price of the product, because consumers will be more likely to pay a high price for a unique product. This may lead to increased revenues, which may result in the business's profit margin increasing.

(Total for Question 3 = 15 marks)
TOTAL FOR SECTION A = 35 MARKS

Writing a good answer

'Discuss' questions will ask you to look at a likely impact, benefit, drawback or similar.

In a 'Discuss' question you should:
- show your **Knowledge and Understanding (AO1)** by giving one or two clear points
- include a minimum of five linked development points across the 1–2 points you have made, to demonstrate your **Analysis (AO3a)**.

A very strong answer because...

✓ **Understanding**: There are two valid points (making the product stand out from the competition; adding value).
✓ **Analysis**: There are six linked strands of development, which more than covers the requirement for a minimum of five. There is also good use of connectives, such as 'This means that' and 'which may result in', to show these links.

SECTION B
Answer ALL questions.
Read the following extract carefully and then answer Questions 4, 5 and 6.
Write your answers in the spaces provided.

Subway® is the world's largest submarine sandwich chain with more than 42 500 locations around the world, and over 2 500 locations in the United Kingdom. Subway has become the leading choice for people seeking quick personalised meals that the whole family can enjoy. In creating the sandwiches, Subway produces sandwiches made to order (job production); the customer can choose the type of bread and salad items that go into their 'Sub'.

Recently, Subway has reviewed its Corporate Social Responsibility (ethical) policies in a number of areas and has made a commitment to be a socially responsible business. For instance, it has stated its commitment in helping to tackle childhood obesity, by taking on the challenge to reduce sugar found in Subway products and in the ingredients provided by third party suppliers. It has also recently been the proud recipient of an award from Compassion in Farming for its commitment to using only free range eggs in all Subway products across Europe.

Demand for Subway products is growing and to ensure that the needs of customers are met, Subway has recently trialled delivery through Just Eat. The world-famous 'Subs' can now be ordered through both the Just Eat app and website, from 1 030 stores across the UK including over 450 stores in London, Leeds and Manchester*. 'Sub' fans can order at any time of the day, including weekends, for delivery to a location of their choice.

The arrival of Subway on the third party apps follows in the footsteps of other favourites including KFC and Burger King, which both joined Just Eat last year.

*correct as of January 2020.

(Adapted from: https://www.subway.com/PressReleases/Subway%20trials%20delivery%20 with%20Just%20Eat.pdf and https://www.subway.com/en-GB/AboutUs/SocialResponsibility/ NutritionalLeadership)

---

4 (a) Outline **one** benefit to *Subway* of behaving ethically. (2)

Behaving ethically will help to improve Subway's brand image. ✓ As a result they may sell more sandwiches. ✓

(b) Analyse the impact on *Subway* of its decision to sell its sandwiches through *Just Eat*. (6)

By selling through the popular takeaway delivery company Just Eat, Subway may be able to reach more potential customers. This is because people who want a quick meal delivery can access Subway's sandwich and salad range through the Just Eat app. This could lead to more sales for Subway and therefore potentially more revenue coming into the food retailer.

Another impact is that selling through Just Eat may be more expensive for Subway than selling direct, as they will have to pay fees to Just Eat in order for them to provide the delivery service. This will push up total costs for Subway, which may result in reduced profit margins, meaning that Subway may become less competitive in the fast food market compared to rivals such as Burger King.

(Total for Question 4 = 8 marks)

Writing a good answer

'Analyse' questions will ask you to look at an impact, advantage, drawback or similar. In an 'Analyse' question you should:
- clearly **apply your answer to the context** throughout (AO2)
- give one or two clear points and a minimum of five linked development points, to demonstrate your **Analysis (AO3a)**.

A very strong answer because...

✓ **Application**: There are multiple references to the market that *Subway* and *Just Eat* operate in, such as 'takeaway delivery', 'quick meal', '*Just Eat app*', 'fast food' and '*Burger King*'.
✓ **Analysis**: There are more than the required minimum of five linked development points.

---

5 Figure 3 shows the number of outlets and total revenue for the top 10 UK restaurant operators in 2017.

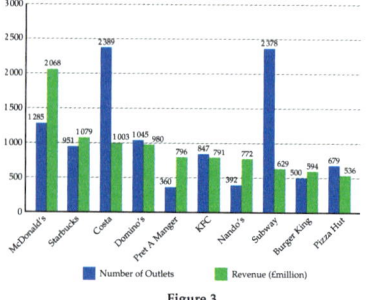

Figure 3

(a) Using the information in Figure 3, calculate the average revenue, to the nearest pound, per *Subway* outlet in 2017. You are advised to show your workings. (2)

$$\text{Average revenue} = \frac{\text{Total revenue}}{\text{Total number of outlets}}$$

$$= \frac{£629\,000\,000}{2378}$$

$$= £264\,508 ✓$$

£264 508 ✓

(b) Using the information in Figure 3, calculate, to two decimal places, *Subway's* revenue as a percentage of the total market revenue of the top 10 restaurants. You are advised to show your workings. (2)

$$\% \text{ of total market share} = \frac{\text{Subway's revenue}}{\text{Total market revenue}} \times 100$$

Total revenue of market (£) = 2068 + 1079 + 1003 + 980 + 796 + 791 + 772 + 629 + 594 + 536
= £9248 m

Subway's revenue = £629 million

$$\% \text{ of total market share} = \frac{£629 m}{£9248 m} \times 100\%$$

$$= 6.80\% ✓$$

6.80 % ✓

Subway uses a system of job production to make each sandwich.

(c) Analyse the benefit to *Subway* of using job production. (6)

Using job production allows Subway to meet the needs of individual customers. This is because the customer can choose which bread and salad items they want. This will lead to customers being more satisfied than if they were to have a pre-packed sandwich, which will help increase sales of the fast food outlet, leading to an increased market share compared to Subway's rivals such as Pret A Manger.

Because Subway will have added more value by allowing the customers to choose the ingredients, the sandwich store will be able to charge a higher price for their sandwiches. This will reduce the number of sandwiches each restaurant has to sell in order to break even, therefore increasing the chances of success for each Subway outlet.

(Total for Question 5 = 10 marks)

Writing a good answer

'Analyse' questions will ask you to look at an impact, advantage, drawback or similar. In an 'Analyse' question you should:
- clearly **apply your answer to the context** throughout your answer (AO2)
- give one or two clear points and a minimum of five linked development points, to demonstrate your **Analysis (AO3a)**.

A very strong answer because...

✓ **Application**: There are references throughout to the market that *Subway* operates in: for example, 'bread and salad items', 'pre-packed sandwich', 'fast food outlet', '*Pret A Manger*'.
✓ **Analysis**: This answer demonstrates the two-paragraph approach. The student has used connectives well, and they have more than the required minimum of five linked development points.

130

Set 1 Paper 2 Answers

6 (a) State **one** benefit to *Subway* of having more than 42 500 locations worldwide. (1)

The sandwich chain's brand will be more recognisable worldwide. ✓

(b) Outline the drawback to *Subway* of using quantitative data to help make decisions. (2)

One drawback is that quantitative data identifies trends that may not continue. ✓ Therefore, Subway may make decisions based on a prediction of an increase in sandwich sales, which may not actually happen. ✓

Currently *Subway* operates a centralised management system in its restaurants. To help it continue to be more competitive in the fast food restaurant market, *Subway* is considering the following two options.

Option 1: Continue with a system of centralisation for all outlets.
Option 2: Introduce a decentralised structure, giving autonomy to outlet managers.

(c) Justify which **one** of these two options *Subway* should choose. (9)

I believe that Subway should continue to have a centralised structure for its restaurants, because there will be uniformity in every outlet. This will allow the sandwich store to continue to be committed to being a socially responsible business. In addition, it will mean that all stores continue to use ethically sourced ingredients, such as free-range eggs. This might not happen in a decentralised structure, for example if individual managers want to cut costs.

However, being centralised doesn't allow individual restaurant managers to meet the needs of local people, as they have to sell certain products at a certain price dictated by head office. This may mean that individual restaurants fail to satisfy their customers fully, which could lead to a fall in competitiveness against other sandwich chains, as customers start to buy food from restaurants that better meet their needs. This may cause Subway's revenues and profits to start to fall.

In conclusion, I believe that centralisation is better for Subway. A customer will want to know that a sandwich they buy in Manchester is exactly the same quality as a sandwich they purchase in London. More importantly, as the customer can individualise their sandwich (by choosing the bread and salad items) their individual needs will be met anyway. However, how successful centralisation is will depend on customer expectations: if customers expect the quality of sandwiches to be the same then centralisation is the best way; if they prefer to buy local speciality sandwiches in different parts of the UK (and globally) then decentralisation may actually be more beneficial for the fast food chain.

(Total for Question 6 = 12 marks)
TOTAL FOR SECTION B = 30 MARKS

Writing a good answer

'Justify' questions will ask you to make a choice between two options. **There is no need to discuss both options.**

When answering a 'Justify' question, aim to write three paragraphs.

- **Paragraph 1:** Select the option you feel is best and state why, using at least three linked strands of development to demonstrate **Analysis (AO3a)**. Make sure you refer to the context throughout, to demonstrate **Application (AO2)**.
- **Paragraph 2:** Explain a drawback of the option you have chosen, to show balance and **Evaluation (AO3b)**. Again, include at least three linked strands of development to demonstrate **Analysis (AO3a)**, and refer to context to demonstrate **Application (AO2)**.
- **Paragraph 3:** Conclude by giving the main reason why you selected your option. Use the 'It depends' rule. This is another way of demonstrating **Evaluation (AO3b)**, and should also refer to the context for **Application (AO2)**.

A very strong answer because...

- **Application:** The case study is referred to in detail throughout. For example, the first paragraph refers to *Subway's* socially responsible behaviour, and the second paragraph makes repeated references to a fall in the sandwich market.
- **Analysis:** There are seven linked strands of development across the first two paragraphs, which more than covers the minimum of five linked strands of development. There is effective use of connectives, such as 'however' and 'this may mean', to demonstrate these links.
- **Evaluation:** This is a balanced argument that considers one advantage and one disadvantage of continuing with a centralised structure. The conclusion is logical and clearly states the main reason why Option 1 has been chosen. Further credit will also be given for effective use of the 'It depends' rule.

SECTION C
Answer ALL questions.
Read the following extract carefully and then answer Question 7.
Write your answers in the spaces provided.

Makeup for men is becoming mainstream.

Chanel is a high fashion and beauty house that specialises in ready-to-wear clothes, luxury goods and fashion accessories.

The French fashion and beauty company is well-known for its extensive range of makeup for women, but in September 2018 it broke new ground by launching a makeup range aimed solely at men. Its new 'Boy de Chanel' range was launched with only a few products initially: an almost imperceptible lip balm, a tinted foundation, and an eyebrow pencil in various shades. These makeup products mark a new addition to the company's 'Boy' division, which has sold perfume and handbags for men since 2015.

As part of its launch, *Chanel* will conduct a product trial in South Korea (as this is the country with the highest demand and advancement in terms of makeup routines for men) before making them available on its website, www.chanel.com, and then eventually in *Chanel* stores worldwide.

When launching the product in Korea, *Chanel* will focus heavily on promotion and has lined up a famous Korean actor and model, Lee Dong Wook, to be the face of the 'Boy de Chanel' line. *Chanel* believes that this strategy of using celebrity endorsement will be particularly key to success when launching the product in Western markets. While this is a new venture for *Chanel*, other brands such as *Clinique* and *MMUK* already offer products designed for men, but by approaching specific celebrities to endorse its products, *Chanel's* may just be differentiated enough to have a competitive advantage.

(Source: https://uk.fashionnetwork.com/news/Chanel-to-launch-a-line-of-makeup-for-men,1006103.html#.XGyTzfZ2uUk and https://www.forbes.com/sites/tiffanyleigh/2018/08/27/chanel-debuts-boy-de-chanel-male-makeup-collection/#6c52ac8ee3c5)

---

7 (a) Define the term **product trial**. (1)

A product trial is when a consumer buys a product for the first time to assess whether or not they want to continue to buy it in future. ✓

Chanel's sales for 2018 totalled $9.62 billion, which represented an 11 per cent increase from the previous year.

(b) Calculate, to two decimal places, the value of *Chanel's* sales in 2017. You are advised to show your workings. (2)

$$2017 \text{ figure} = \frac{\text{original figure}}{1.11\%}$$
$$= \frac{9.62}{1.11} = 8.67 \checkmark$$
$$\$8.67 \text{ billion} \checkmark$$

(c) State **one** element of the sales process that will be important in helping *Chanel* provide a good level of customer service. (1)

One element would be customer engagement through the sales staff having good knowledge of the makeup that is being sold. ✓

To help its new makeup range to sell successfully, *Chanel* is considering two options to motivate its sales staff.

Option 1: Offering sales staff commission on the sales they make.
Option 2: Providing job enrichment by involving sales staff in the launch of the new range.

(d) Justify which **one** of these two options *Chanel* should choose. (9)

I think Chanel should choose Option 1, because money is a big motivator for a lot of people. Therefore, the sales staff would work extremely hard to sell the new makeup range, because the more cosmetics they sell, the more money the sales staff would make. This would benefit the cosmetic company, as it would potentially sell more lip balms, foundations and eyebrow pencils, resulting in increased sales and therefore a competitive advantage over rivals such as Clinique and MMUK.

However, it would be expensive for Chanel to offer its sales staff commission on sales of the new beauty range, because the average cost of selling each lip balm would increase. This might mean that Chanel has to sell the makeup range at a higher price, which may deter men from buying the beauty products in favour of cheaper makeup from Clinique, potentially causing the launch to be unsuccessful.

Ultimately, the decision will depend on what actually motivates the sales assistants. If financial rewards are most important to them, then offering commission on the sales of makeup will be vital to the success of the product launch. However, if sales assistants want to feel valued and part of the launch of the beauty products then giving them some responsibility in the launch may be more effective.

131

Set 1 Paper 2 Answers

Writing a good answer

'Justify' questions will ask you to make a choice between two options. **There is no need to discuss both options.**

When answering a 'Justify' question, aim to write three paragraphs.

- **Paragraph 1:** Select the option you feel is best and state why, using at least three linked strands of development to demonstrate **Analysis (AO3a)**. Make sure you refer to the context throughout, to demonstrate **Application (AO2)**.
- **Paragraph 2:** Explain a drawback of the option you have chosen, to show balance and **Evaluation (AO3b)**. Again, include at least three linked strands of development to demonstrate **Analysis (AO3a)**, and refer to context to demonstrate **Application (AO2)**.
  By including three linked strands of development in both paragraphs, you can be more confident that you are covering the overall requirement of five linked strands of development for this answer.
- **Paragraph 3:** Conclude by giving the main reason why you selected your option. Use the 'It depends' rule. This is another way of demonstrating **Evaluation (AO3b)**, and should also refer to the context for **Application (AO2)**.

A very strong answer because...

✓ **Application:** In all three paragraphs, repeated references are made to the male makeup and cosmetics industry. Information from the case study is used to support the response well.

✓ **Analysis:** In each of the first two paragraphs there are three or four linked strands of development. This means there is more than the required minimum of five linked development points.

✓ **Evaluation:** The response is balanced, and in the conclusion, value is placed on the argument by saying what is 'vital' if the launch is to be successful. There is also effective use of the 'It depends' rule.

(e) Evaluate whether promotion will be the most important component of the marketing mix in contributing to the successful launch of *Chanel's* new products. You should use the information provided as well as your knowledge of business. (12)

The marketing mix is a combination of factors (price, product, place and promotion) that a business uses to persuade customers to buy its products – in this case, that Chanel uses to persuade customers to buy its new makeup for men.

Promotion is incredibly important to the successful launch of the French beauty house's makeup range, as it informs potential customers (in South Korea in the first instance) that the products are available. By using celebrity endorsements by famous models and actors such as Lee Dong Wook, Chanel can ensure that potential customers notice the new products, which may result in healthy sales of lip balms, eyebrow pencils and foundation. This could help the cosmetics firm to become established in the male makeup market, allowing Chanel to then move into other geographical areas and to sell online via www.chanel.com.

However, it could be argued that the product element of the marketing mix is more important than promotion. This is because, if the quality of the makeup is poor, customers would very quickly start to purchase products from rival businesses such as Clinique and MMUK. This would mean sales of Chanel's male beauty products would be insufficient for the company to break even (even if the products are endorsed by celebrities), meaning that Chanel would have wasted a lot of money on an unsuccessful launch.

In this case I believe that promotion is possibly the most important element, particularly in the short term. The male makeup market is a new market segment for Chanel, and it has to let men know that makeup is available to them. Customers will be encouraged to purchase the eyebrow pencils, foundation and lip balm if they see celebrities such as Lee Dong Wook using them, so promotion is crucial.

However, for sustained success, Chanel will need an integrated marketing mix that is carefully considered, because while promotion will get people to buy the makeup initially, if it is not deemed to be good enough in terms of quality, then no one will continue to buy it.

(Total for Question 7 = 25 marks)
TOTAL FOR SECTION C = 25 MARKS
TOTAL FOR PAPER = 90 MARKS

Writing a good answer

In an 'Evaluate' question you should aim for three paragraphs.

- **Paragraph 1:** Show your **Knowledge and Understanding (AO1)**; for example, give a definition of one of the key terms and use Business terms throughout. Then provide arguments in support of the statement, with at least three linked development points to show thorough **Analysis (AO3a)**. Include the context throughout (AO2).
- **Paragraph 2:** Give alternative arguments, with at least three linked development points to show thorough **Analysis (AO3a)**. Apply your points to the context throughout (AO2).
  By including three linked strands of development in both paragraphs, you can be more confident that you are covering the overall requirement of five linked strands for this answer.
- **Paragraph 3:** Give a balanced conclusion to demonstrate your **Evaluation (AO3b)**, making use of the 'It depends' argument.

A very strong answer because...

✓ **Understanding:** The response starts with a clear definition of the marketing mix, demonstrating excellent Knowledge and Understanding. Business terminology is used correctly.

✓ **Application:** There is excellent use of the case study in each paragraph, for example the importance of using the celebrity Lee Dong Wook to promote the product.

✓ **Analysis:** Paragraphs 1 and 2 each contain at least three linked strands of development. There is excellent use of connectives such as 'however' and 'this would mean' to demonstrate these links.

✓ **Evaluation:** The balanced argument explains why promotion is the most important element but also suggests why another element of the marketing mix is essential to the success of *Chanel's* new makeup range. The conclusion details why promotion is significant in the short term, but also the importance of an integrated marketing mix to achieve sustained success.

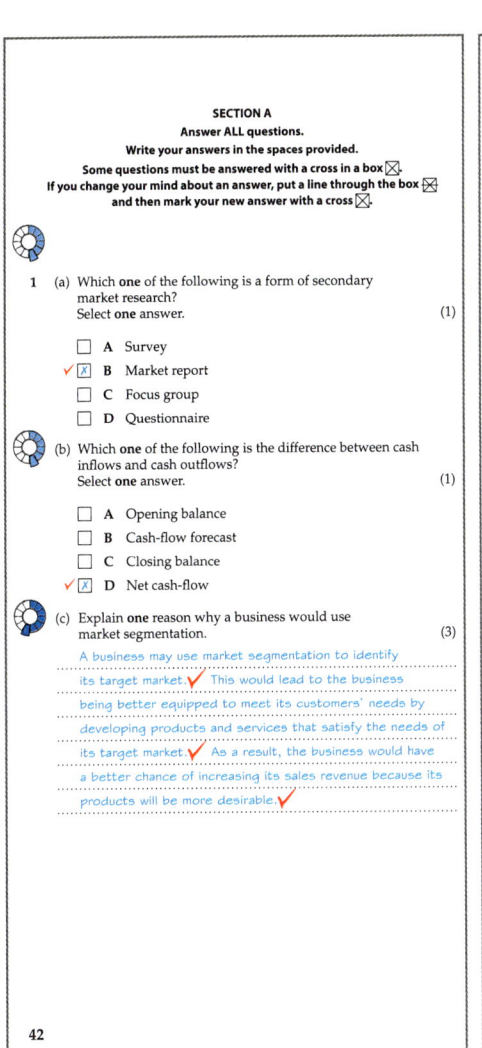

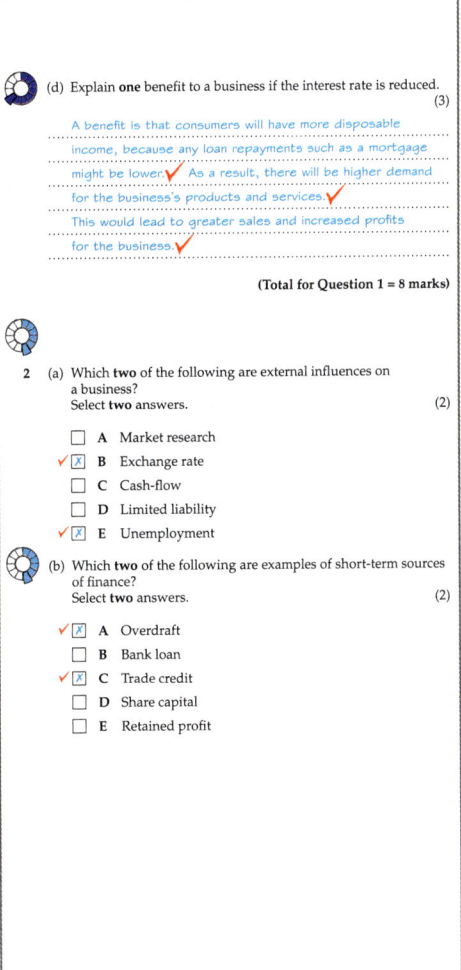

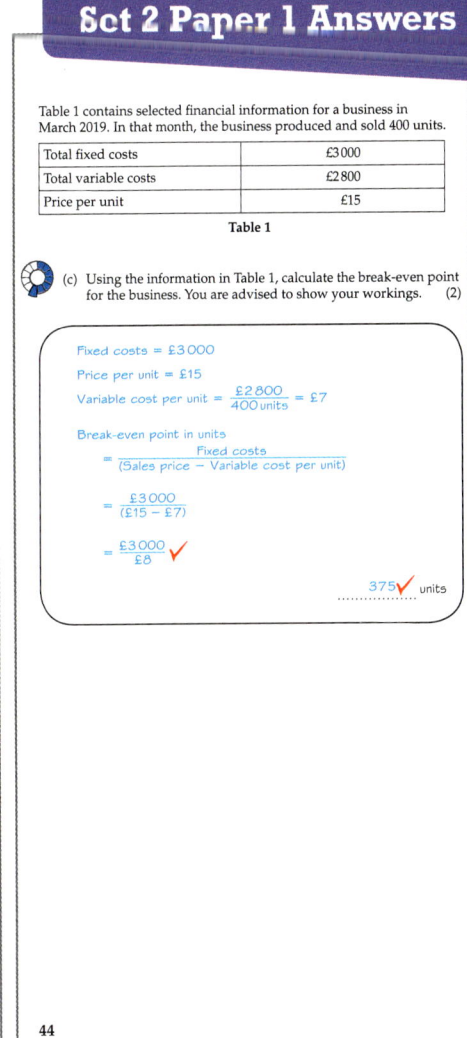

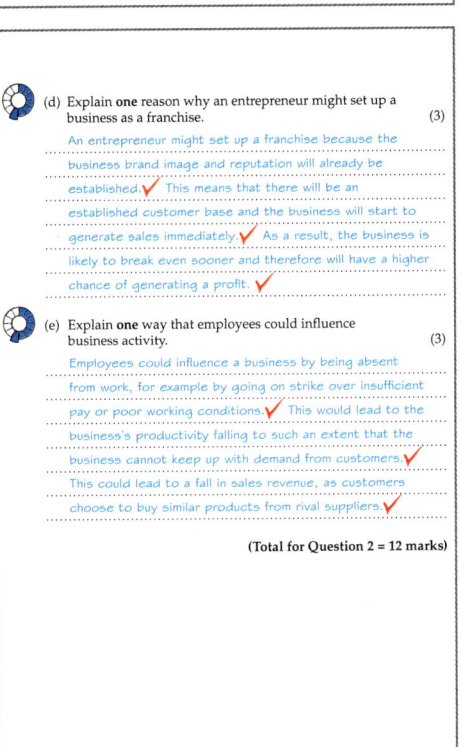

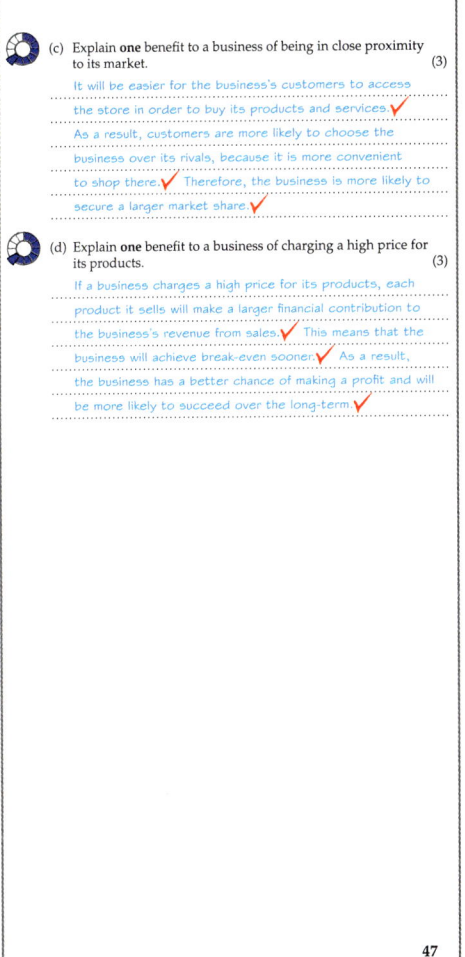

Set 2 Paper 1 Answers

SECTION A
Answer ALL questions.
Write your answers in the spaces provided.
Some questions must be answered with a cross in a box ☒.
If you change your mind about an answer, put a line through the box ☒ and then mark your new answer with a cross ☒.

1 (a) Which **one** of the following is a form of secondary market research?
Select **one** answer. (1)

- ☐ A Survey
- ☒ B Market report ✓
- ☐ C Focus group
- ☐ D Questionnaire

(b) Which **one** of the following is the difference between cash inflows and cash outflows?
Select **one** answer. (1)

- ☐ A Opening balance
- ☐ B Cash-flow forecast
- ☐ C Closing balance
- ☒ D Net cash-flow ✓

(c) Explain **one** reason why a business would use market segmentation. (3)

A business may use market segmentation to identify its target market. ✓ This would lead to the business being better equipped to meet its customers' needs by developing products and services that satisfy the needs of its target market. ✓ As a result, the business would have a better chance of increasing its sales revenue because its products will be more desirable. ✓

(d) Explain **one** benefit to a business if the interest rate is reduced. (3)

A benefit is that consumers will have more disposable income, because any loan repayments such as a mortgage might be lower. ✓ As a result, there will be higher demand for the business's products and services. ✓ This would lead to greater sales and increased profits for the business. ✓

(Total for Question 1 = 8 marks)

2 (a) Which **two** of the following are external influences on a business?
Select **two** answers. (2)

- ☐ A Market research
- ☒ B Exchange rate ✓
- ☐ C Cash-flow
- ☐ D Limited liability
- ☒ E Unemployment ✓

(b) Which **two** of the following are examples of short-term sources of finance?
Select **two** answers. (2)

- ☒ A Overdraft ✓
- ☐ B Bank loan
- ☒ C Trade credit ✓
- ☐ D Share capital
- ☐ E Retained profit

(d) Explain **one** reason why an entrepreneur might set up a business as a franchise. (3)

An entrepreneur might set up a franchise because the business brand image and reputation will already be established. ✓ This means that there will be an established customer base and the business will start to generate sales immediately. ✓ As a result, the business is likely to break even sooner and therefore will have a higher chance of generating a profit. ✓

(e) Explain **one** way that employees could influence business activity. (3)

Employees could influence a business by being absent from work, for example by going on strike over insufficient pay or poor working conditions. ✓ This would lead to the business's productivity falling to such an extent that the business cannot keep up with demand from customers. ✓ This could lead to a fall in sales revenue, as customers choose to buy similar products from rival suppliers. ✓

(Total for Question 2 = 12 marks)

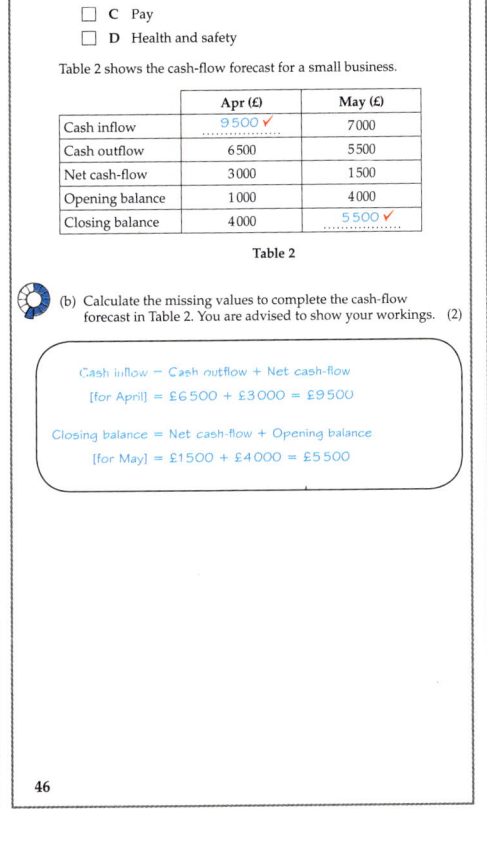

3 (a) Which **one** of the following is **not** covered by employment law?
Select **one** answer. (1)

- ☐ A Recruitment
- ☒ B Product quality ✓
- ☐ C Pay
- ☐ D Health and safety

Table 2 shows the cash-flow forecast for a small business.

	Apr (£)	May (£)
Cash inflow	9500 ✓	7000
Cash outflow	6500	5500
Net cash-flow	3000	1500
Opening balance	1000	4000
Closing balance	4000	5500 ✓

Table 2

(b) Calculate the missing values to complete the cash-flow forecast in Table 2. You are advised to show your workings. (2)

Cash inflow = Cash outflow + Net cash-flow
[for April] = £6500 + £3000 = £9500

Closing balance = Net cash-flow + Opening balance
[for May] = £1500 + £4000 = £5500

Table 1 contains selected financial information for a business in March 2019. In that month, the business produced and sold 400 units.

Total fixed costs	£3000
Total variable costs	£2800
Price per unit	£15

Table 1

(c) Using the information in Table 1, calculate the break-even point for the business. You are advised to show your workings. (2)

Fixed costs = £3000
Price per unit = £15
Variable cost per unit = $\frac{£2800}{400 \text{ units}}$ = £7

Break-even point in units
$= \frac{\text{Fixed costs}}{(\text{Sales price} - \text{Variable cost per unit})}$

$= \frac{£3000}{(£15 - £7)}$

$= \frac{£3000}{£8}$ ✓

= 375 ✓ units

(c) Explain **one** benefit to a business of being in close proximity to its market. (3)

It will be easier for the business's customers to access the store in order to buy its products and services. ✓ As a result, customers are more likely to choose the business over its rivals, because it is more convenient to shop there. ✓ Therefore, the business is more likely to secure a larger market share. ✓

(d) Explain **one** benefit to a business of charging a high price for its products. (3)

If a business charges a high price for its products, each product it sells will make a larger financial contribution to the business's revenue from sales. ✓ This means that the business will achieve break-even sooner. ✓ As a result, the business has a better chance of making a profit and will be more likely to succeed over the long-term. ✓

133

Set 2 Paper 1 Answers

(e) Discuss the role of entrepreneurship in setting up a successful business. (6)

Successful businesses are created because entrepreneurs are willing to take risks to invest their own capital. Setting up a new business is risky (around 40% of new businesses fail) – so without risk-taking, no new businesses would be established. By taking risks, entrepreneurs take the opportunity to supply goods and services where there is a gap in the market. As a result, entrepreneurs help ensure people's wants and needs are satisfied.

Another role of entrepreneurship is to make business decisions. This might include generating new ideas. New business ideas can lead to new business opportunities through creative products and services. Creative products and services can help a business differentiate its offering from those of its competitors and stand out in the market, therefore increasing the potential that more customers will choose its products, so increasing its market share.

(Total for Question 3 = 15 marks)
TOTAL FOR SECTION A = 35 MARKS

Writing a good answer

'Discuss' questions will ask you to look at a likely impact, benefit, drawback or similar.
In a 'Discuss' question you should:
- show your **Knowledge and Understanding (AO1)** by giving one or two clear points
- include a minimum of five linked development points across the 1–2 points you have made, to demonstrate your **Analysis (AO3a)**.

A very strong answer because…

✓ **Understanding**: Two valid features or characteristics of an entrepreneur have been identified (willingness to take risks and ability to make business decisions).

✓ **Analysis**: There are six linked strands of development, which more than covers the requirement for a minimum of five. There is good use of connectives, such as 'as a result', 'therefore' and 'can lead to', to show these links.

SECTION B
Answer ALL questions.
Read the following extract carefully and then answer Questions 4, 5 and 6.
Write your answers in the spaces provided.

After leaving college six years ago, Rob decided he had the skills and experience to set up his own gardening and landscape design business, *Down To Earth*, as a sole trader.

Rob had identified a gap in the market for a budget gardening service that could also offer a free garden design service. Many of the larger gardening companies Rob had come across charge a premium for detailed garden designs and consultancy. Rob planned to offer this service for free and use new technology to provide his customers with high-quality 3D designs of their new gardens.

Rob's market research into the local garden design and landscaping market found that there was little difference between competitors in terms of the service they provided. However, the largest competitor in the local area, *Olive Tree Gardens Ltd*, promoted its excellent customer service on its website.

In order to finance his own start-up, Rob estimated he would require £15 000. He invested £6000 of his own savings and secured the remainder of the investment through a bank loan. As part of his application, Rob produced a detailed business plan.

In order that *Down to Earth* could establish a reputation for providing a premium service at a budget price, Rob decided to charge a price 25 per cent lower than the average competitor for *Down to Earth*'s gardening and landscaping services.

---

4 (a) Outline **one** benefit to Rob of producing a business plan for *Down to Earth*. (2)

By producing a business plan, Rob was able to demonstrate that he understood the gardening and landscape design business and market. ✓ As a result, he was able to secure a £9000 bank loan. ✓

(b) Analyse the impact on Rob of setting up *Down to Earth* as a sole trader. (6)

As a sole trader, Rob can start his gardening and landscape design business without the cost and hassle of setting up a private limited company. This means he could start Down to Earth quickly, therefore maximising the opportunity to exploit the gap in the market for a budget gardening service as soon as possible and begin competing with other businesses such as Olive Tree Gardens Ltd. As Rob is just starting out, he might want to keep his gardening business simple initially, to determine whether he can succeed before setting up a private limited company in the future.

Another impact is that by operating as a sole trader, Rob would not have to publish his financial accounts – they would remain private. This would mean his competitors and customers would not be able to view his accounts to find out any trading information. Therefore, competitors could not use this information to their benefit, such as trying to understand how profitable his budget gardening and landscaping service is. This is an advantage Rob would have over his competitor Olive Tree Gardens Ltd, which as a private limited company does need to make its financial accounts available for public view.

(Total for Question 4 = 8 marks)

---

5 Rob signed up his first customer in June. After the design service, Rob provided the customer with a materials estimate of £1300 and a labour estimate of £1500. In order to provide the customer with a final price, he needed to then apply the introductory discount of 25 per cent.

(a) Using the information above, calculate the total price after discount that the customer paid. (2)

Total price = £1300 + £1500 = £2800

Total price after 25% discount = Total price × 0.75
= £2800 × 0.75
= £2100 ✓

£2100 ✓

In July, Rob completed three garden projects for different customers. Table 3 shows *Down to Earth*'s costs and revenue for that month.

Fixed costs	£400
Average variable costs per garden project	£700
Average revenue per garden project	£1600

Table 3

(b) Using the information in Table 3, calculate the total profit Rob made in July. (2)

Total revenue for 3 garden projects = £1600 × 3 = £4800

Average variable costs for 3 garden projects = £700 × 3
= £2100

Total costs = Fixed costs + total variable costs
= £400 + £2100 = £2500

Profit = Total revenue − Total costs
= £4800 − £2500 = £2300 ✓

£2300 ✓

(c) Analyse the impact on *Down to Earth* of charging a price 25 per cent lower than the average competitor for the first six months. (6)

One impact is that Rob is likely to attract new customers to his start-up gardening business, because his prices will be lower than his competitors'. This will be benefit Rob because his sole trader business is not yet established, so he needs to build a reputation for providing a quality budget gardening service. If Rob can impress the first garden design customers he attracts, he will have a greater chance of generating sufficient revenue within the first six months to help his business break even.

Another impact on Down to Earth's gardening and landscaping services is that Rob could struggle with his cash-flow. Setting up a business can be expensive and Rob will have many outgoings, such as the costs for gardening tools. Rob is offering new customers a considerably lower price over the first six months, which means his cash inflows may not cover the cash outflows over this period. As a result, Rob may have to keep back some of the £15 000 investment in order to help manage his cash-flow. This means that he will have less money available to market his new services.

(Total for Question 5 = 10 marks)

Writing a good answer

In an 'Analyse' question you should:
- **apply your answer to the context** throughout (AO2)
- give one or two clear points and a minimum of five linked development points, to demonstrate your **Analysis (AO3a)**.

A very strong answer because…

✓ **Analysis**: There are two valid points (a lower price will attract new customers but limit Rob's cash inflows), which are supported by six linked development points and effective use of connectives.

✓ **Application**: Reference to the case study is made throughout the answer, for example 'gardening and landscaping services', 'within the first six months', '£15 000 investment', 'sole trader'.

---

6 (a) State **one** reason why Rob might have decided to start his own business. (1)

He would gain personal satisfaction from successfully running his own gardening and landscape design business. ✓

(b) Outline **one** benefit to Rob of using new technology in his business. (2)

By using garden design software to provide high-quality 3D designs, Rob will be able to communicate his landscaping ideas better to his customers. ✓ This could help improve his customers' experience, meaning they are more likely to recommend his gardening and landscape design business to others. ✓

134

Set 2 Paper 1 Answers

Rob is considering two options to increase revenue for *Down to Earth*.
Option 1: Advertise *Down to Earth* on the local radio.
Option 2: Give customers a £50 voucher if a recommendation from them leads to a new contract.

(c) Justify which **one** of these two options Rob should choose. (9)

If Rob promotes his gardening and landscape design business by advertising on the local radio, many potential customers in the local area may hear the advert. As a result, they may get in touch with Rob for a quote for his budget gardening service. As Rob is offering all new customers a lower price, many of these queries may be turned into actual customers. Therefore, advertising on the radio may help Rob generate lots of new business in his first six months of trading, especially if the radio advert highlights the fact that his prices are 25 per cent lower than most competitors.

However, not everyone who is looking for gardening and landscaping services will listen to the local radio station. This means that Rob could lose out on potential customers if he does not use a variety of strategies to promote his business, such as print media and social media. Therefore, just advertising on the local radio could mean that it takes longer for Down to Earth to become an established gardening business in the local area than if Rob used a variety of forms of promotion.

In conclusion, the local radio advert is a better option than offering £50 garden vouchers to customers who have recommended Down to Earth's gardening services leading to a new contract. As Rob is just starting out as a sole trader, he does not have many customers, and the £50 voucher scheme means he would be reliant on only a handful of existing customers to generate new customers for him. It is much better for Rob to increase local awareness of his budget gardening business through advertising. However, the success of the radio advert may depend on the number of listeners the radio station has and the price of the advert in comparison to other advertising mediums, such as the local newspaper.

(Total for Question 6 = 12 marks)
TOTAL FOR SECTION B = 30 MARKS

Writing a good answer

'Justify' questions will ask you to make a choice between two options. There is no need to discuss both options.

When answering a 'Justify' question, aim to write three paragraphs.
- **Paragraph 1:** Select the option you feel is best and state why, using at least three linked strands of development to demonstrate **Analysis (AO3a)**. Make sure you refer to the context throughout, to demonstrate **Application (AO2)**.
- **Paragraph 2:** Explain a drawback of the option you have chosen, to show balance and **Evaluation (AO3b)**. Again, include at least three linked strands of development to demonstrate **Analysis (AO3a)**, and refer to context to demonstrate **Application (AO2)**.
By including three linked strands of development in both paragraphs, you can be more confident that you are covering the overall requirement of five linked strands of development for this answer.
- **Paragraph 3:** Conclude by giving the main reason why you selected your option. Use the 'It depends' rule. This is another way of demonstrating **Evaluation (AO3b)**, and should also refer to the context for **Application (AO2)**.

A very strong answer because...

✓ **Application:** In all three paragraphs, repeated references are made to Rob's garden and landscape design business. Information from the case study – for example, about the lower price and garden design technology – is used to support the response well.
✓ **Analysis:** Across the first two paragraphs there are at least five linked strands of development. There is also excellent use of connectives, such as 'as a result', 'however' and 'this means that', to show these links.
✓ **Evaluation:** The response is balanced, giving one benefit and then one drawback of the chosen option. The conclusion emphasises what is most important if Rob's promotion of *Down to Earth* is to successfully generate more revenue for the business. There is also effective use of the 'It depends' rule in relation to the potential number of radio listeners.

SECTION C
Answer ALL questions.
Read the following extract carefully and then answer Question 7.
Write your answers in the spaces provided.

Rags to Riches manufactures unique bags and accessories from recycled materials. Martha set up the company five years ago when she ran the company from her home. *Rags to Riches* now employs three workers and operates from a small factory where the unique and one-off bags are designed and made.

Martha has always used social media to promote her brand. Every new product is shared on the company's Instagram account; customers can then follow a link to purchase the bag from the *Rags to Riches* website. *Rags to Riches* also sells a small proportion of its products through small independent retailers. Furthermore, 15 per cent of all revenue generated by *Rags to Riches* goes towards helping the homeless buy formal clothing for work.

Most of the materials used to make the bags come from recycled clothing. *Rags to Riches* purchases the clothing in bulk by the ton from collection and recycling companies in order to benefit from a discount on large volumes purchased. Using recycled materials in this way helps *Rags to Riches* to keep its variable costs low, but due to the large volumes purchased, some of the material is not suitable for the bags, with almost 30 per cent of the material going to landfill.

---

7 (a) State **one** fixed cost for *Rags to Riches*. (1)

Mortgage repayments or rent for the small factory from which Martha runs her bags and accessories business. ✓

Figure 1 shows *Rags to Riches*' financial data for 2015–2018.

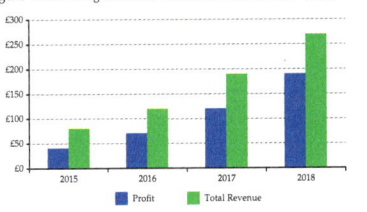

[Bar chart showing Profit and Total Revenue for 2015-2018, with values approximately: 2015 £40/£80, 2016 £70/£110, 2017 £120/£190, 2018 £190/£270]

(b) Identify, using Figure 1, the year when *Rags to Riches*' profit was 50 per cent of total revenue. (1)

2015 ✓

(c) Outline **one** benefit to *Rags to Riches* of manufacturing unique bags for its customers. (2)

Rags to Riches can charge a premium price for producing unique bags made from recycled materials. ✓ This means it can achieve a high profit margin, because using recycled materials helps to keep its variable costs low. ✓

Martha has identified **two** ways that *Rags to Riches* could add value to its products.
Option 1: Improve the quality of each bag.
Option 2: Offer customers the option of having their initials embroidered on the bags.

(d) Justify which **one** of these two options Martha should choose. (9)

If Martha is able to improve the quality of each bag, this would add considerable value because each bag would be more durable and last longer. As each bag is unique, customers will not be able to replace a bag if it wears out or is broken, therefore they will be more satisfied if they believe the bag will last a long time. As a result, improved quality will allow Martha to charge a higher price. This will increase her overall profits, therefore the 15 per cent of profits which Rags to Riches contributes towards helping homeless people buy formal work wear will increase in value, meaning Rags to Riches can support more people to access professional jobs.

However, by improving the quality of each bag, it is likely that variable costs will also rise. Martha may not be able to use recycled materials, or may have to use more material in the production of each bag. This could have the opposite impact of reducing profit margins or lowering overall demand if customers no longer feel that the unique bags are good value for money.

In conclusion, improving the quality of each bag is a better option to add value, as embroidering initials is a simple addition that would have to be done after a sale has been made. Fewer customers are likely to want their initials on the bag, so it would add little value, whereas every customer will appreciate better quality. Overall, the level of value added by improving the quality of each bag will depend on whether Martha can source better-quality recycled materials. Using new material is one way to improve quality, but this would contradict her brand image and USP.

Writing a good answer

'Justify' questions will ask you to make a choice between two options. There is no need to discuss both options.

When answering a 'Justify' question, aim to write three paragraphs.
- **Paragraph 1:** Select the option you feel is best and state why, using at least three linked strands of development to demonstrate **Analysis (AO3a)**. Make sure you refer to the context throughout, to demonstrate **Application (AO2)**.
- **Paragraph 2:** Explain a drawback of the option you have chosen, to show balance and **Evaluation (AO3b)**. Again, include at least three linked strands of development to demonstrate **Analysis (AO3a)**, and refer to **context** to demonstrate **Application (AO2)**.
By including three linked strands of development in both paragraphs, you can be more confident that you are covering the overall requirement of five linked strands of development for this answer.
- **Paragraph 3:** Conclude by giving the main reason why you selected your option. Use the 'It depends' rule. This is another way of demonstrating **Evaluation (AO3b)**, and should also refer to the **context** for **Application (AO2)**.

A very strong answer because...

✓ **Application:** The context of the case study is referred to throughout the answer, including the contribution of 15 per cent of profits to a good cause, unique bags and recycled materials.
✓ **Analysis:** There are six linked strands of development across the first two paragraphs based on the benefits and limitations of Option 1, which is more than the minimum of five linked strands required. There is effective use of connectives, such as 'as a result' and 'it is likely that', to show these links.
✓ **Evaluation:** The answer is balanced: it discusses the benefits and limitations of at least one option, and there is a clear conclusion based on the analysis and supported by strong justification. There is also good use of the 'It depends' rule.

135

Set 2 Paper 1 Answers

Many collection and recycling companies export second-hand clothing in bulk. Due to increased demand from abroad, the cost of buying second-hand clothing has increased by 15 per cent in the last 12 months.

(e) Evaluate whether the rising cost of recycled clothing will impact on the profits of *Rags to Riches*. You should use the information provided as well as your knowledge of business. (12)

The cost of second-hand clothing rising by 15 per cent will have the impact of lowering the profit margins on each bag that Rags to Riches sells. This is because Martha's variable costs will rise, unless she can increase her prices or find a way to reduce other business costs or improve efficiency. For example, if she used more materials from recycling companies, perhaps with only 10 per cent wastage, her variable costs would fall and help protect her profit margin.

Another factor that may have a greater impact on Rags to Riches profits is the level of competition in the fashion market. Most major high street clothing brands also sell a variety of bags. If other brands develop bags that are similar to Martha's then this could reduce demand for her bags and lower her sales and overall profits. However, if Martha can develop the Rags to Riches brand through greater use of social media such as Instagram, this might protect it from competition and help maintain price levels, especially as her bags are unique and support the homeless.

In conclusion, increasing costs of second-hand clothing will reduce profitability, but variable costs are already very low due to the nature of using recycled materials, therefore it might be easy for the business to absorb these costs, such as reducing levels of wastage from 30 per cent or negotiating a better price with Martha's suppliers. However, it is more likely that other factors such as consumer demand and competition will have a greater impact on profits, because the fashion industry is extremely competitive and many customers are becoming conscious of fast fashion and the amount of clothing thrown away each year by top clothing brands. Overall, the extent that the price of second-hand clothing will impact on profits will depend on the fluctuation in price and the quantity (bulk buying) Martha makes, as this could offset the price rise.

(Total for Question 7 = 25 marks)
TOTAL FOR SECTION C = 25 MARKS
TOTAL FOR PAPER = 90 MARKS

Writing a good answer

In an 'Evaluate' question you should aim for three paragraphs.
- **Paragraph 1:** Show your **Knowledge and Understanding (AO1)**; for example, give a definition of one of the key terms and use Business terms throughout. Then provide arguments in support of the statement, with at least three linked development points to show thorough **Analysis (AO3a)**. **Apply your points to the context** in all three paragraphs (AO2).
- **Paragraph 2:** Give alternative arguments, with at least three linked development points to show thorough **Analysis (AO3a)**. By including three linked strands of development in both paragraphs, you can be more confident that you are covering the overall requirement of five linked strands of development.
- **Paragraph 3:** Give a balanced conclusion to demonstrate your **Evaluation (AO3b)**, making use of the 'It depends' argument.

A very strong answer because...

✓ **Understanding:** This answer demonstrates a sound understanding of demand for second-hand clothing and its impact on *Rags to Riches*, as well as business issues such as competition and factors that influence revenue, costs and profit.

✓ **Application:** The answer refers closely to the case study throughout, for example: 30 per cent wastage of raw materials, supporting the homeless, the use of Instagram.

✓ **Analysis:** There are six linked strands of development within the first two paragraphs, which is more than the minimum of five required. There is effective use of connectives to show these links.

✓ **Evaluation:** The answer is balanced, discussing the impact of rising costs as well as other factors that could affect *Rags to Riches*' profits. There is a clear conclusion based on the analysis and a strong justification of why other factors may have a more significant impact on profits with use of the 'It depends' rule.

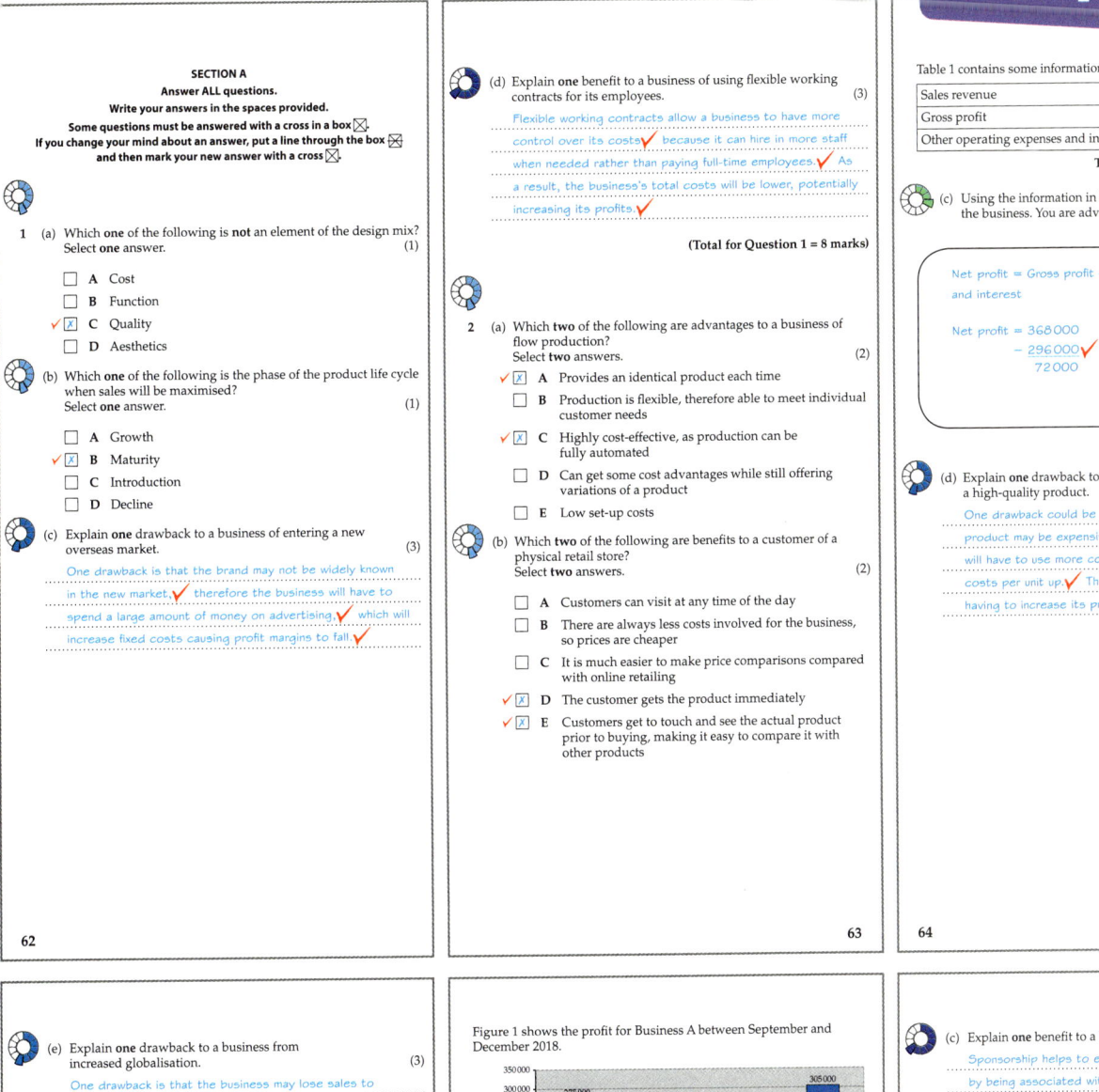

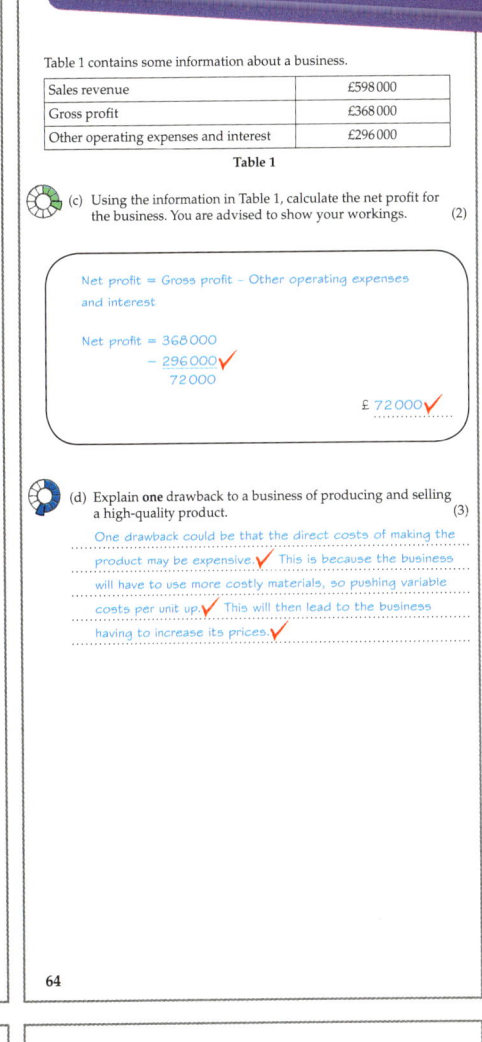

Set 2 Paper 2 Answers

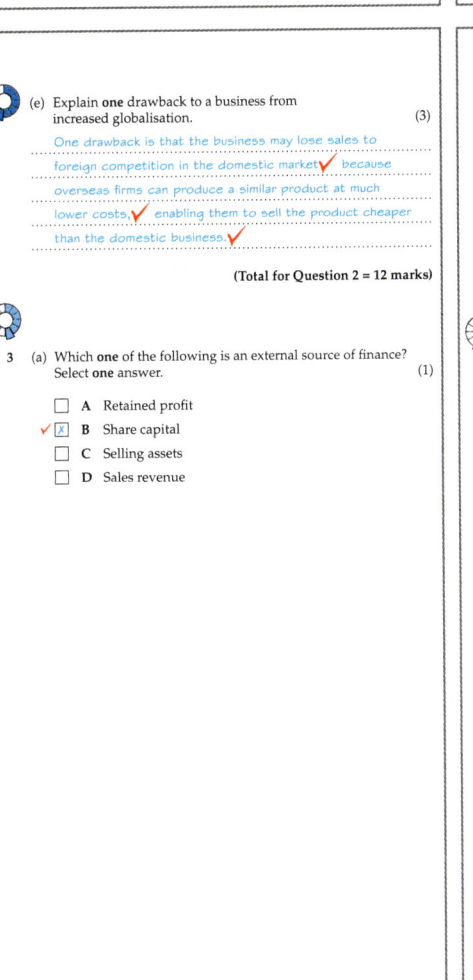

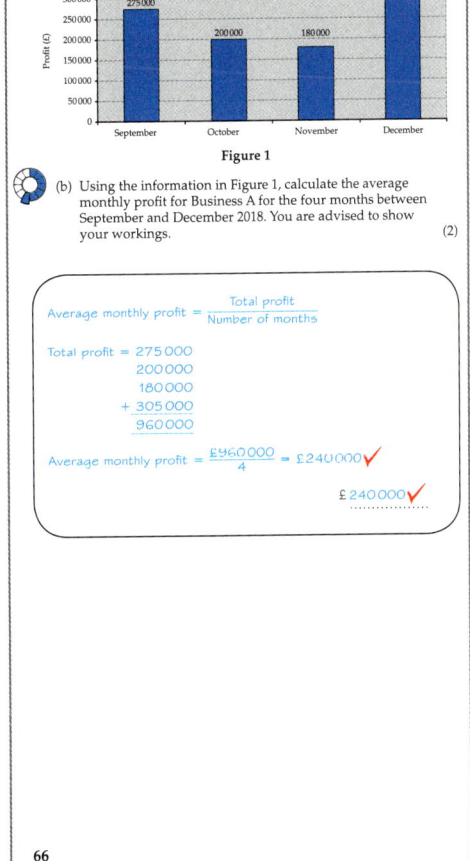

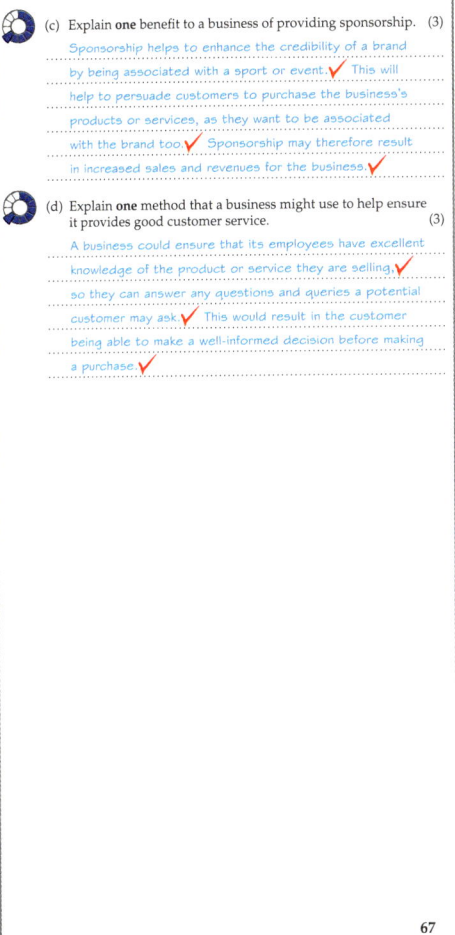

SECTION A
Answer ALL questions.
Write your answers in the spaces provided.
Some questions must be answered with a cross in a box ☒.
If you change your mind about an answer, put a line through the box ☒ and then mark your new answer with a cross ☒.

1 (a) Which **one** of the following is **not** an element of the design mix?
Select **one** answer. (1)

- ☐ A Cost
- ☐ B Function
- ☒ C Quality ✓
- ☐ D Aesthetics

(b) Which **one** of the following is the phase of the product life cycle when sales will be maximised?
Select **one** answer. (1)

- ☐ A Growth
- ☒ B Maturity ✓
- ☐ C Introduction
- ☐ D Decline

(c) Explain **one** drawback to a business of entering a new overseas market. (3)

One drawback is that the brand may not be widely known in the new market, ✓ therefore the business will have to spend a large amount of money on advertising, ✓ which will increase fixed costs causing profit margins to fall. ✓

(d) Explain **one** benefit to a business of using flexible working contracts for its employees. (3)

Flexible working contracts allow a business to have more control over its costs ✓ because it can hire in more staff when needed rather than paying full-time employees. ✓ As a result, the business's total costs will be lower, potentially increasing its profits. ✓

(Total for Question 1 = 8 marks)

2 (a) Which **two** of the following are advantages to a business of flow production?
Select **two** answers. (2)

- ☒ A Provides an identical product each time ✓
- ☐ B Production is flexible, therefore able to meet individual customer needs
- ☒ C Highly cost-effective, as production can be fully automated ✓
- ☐ D Can get some cost advantages while still offering variations of a product
- ☐ E Low set-up costs

(b) Which **two** of the following are benefits to a customer of a physical retail store?
Select **two** answers. (2)

- ☐ A Customers can visit at any time of the day
- ☐ B There are always less costs involved for the business, so prices are cheaper
- ☐ C It is much easier to make price comparisons compared with online retailing
- ☒ D The customer gets the product immediately ✓
- ☒ E Customers get to touch and see the actual product prior to buying, making it easy to compare it with other products ✓

Table 1 contains some information about a business.

Sales revenue	£598 000
Gross profit	£368 000
Other operating expenses and interest	£296 000

Table 1

(c) Using the information in Table 1, calculate the net profit for the business. You are advised to show your workings. (2)

Net profit = Gross profit – Other operating expenses and interest

Net profit = 368 000
 – 296 000 ✓
   72 000

£ 72 000 ✓

(d) Explain **one** drawback to a business of producing and selling a high-quality product. (3)

One drawback could be that the direct costs of making the product may be expensive. ✓ This is because the business will have to use more costly materials, so pushing variable costs per unit up. ✓ This will then lead to the business having to increase its prices. ✓

(e) Explain **one** drawback to a business from increased globalisation. (3)

One drawback is that the business may lose sales to foreign competition in the domestic market ✓ because overseas firms can produce a similar product at much lower costs, ✓ enabling them to sell the product cheaper than the domestic business. ✓

(Total for Question 2 = 12 marks)

3 (a) Which **one** of the following is an external source of finance?
Select **one** answer. (1)

- ☐ A Retained profit
- ☒ B Share capital ✓
- ☐ C Selling assets
- ☐ D Sales revenue

Figure 1 shows the profit for Business A between September and December 2018.

Figure 1
September: 275 000
October: 200 000
November: 180 000
December: 305 000

(b) Using the information in Figure 1, calculate the average monthly profit for Business A for the four months between September and December 2018. You are advised to show your workings. (2)

Average monthly profit = Total profit / Number of months

Total profit = 275 000
 200 000
 180 000
 + 305 000
 960 000

Average monthly profit = £960 000 / 4 = £240 000 ✓

£ 240 000 ✓

(c) Explain **one** benefit to a business of providing sponsorship. (3)

Sponsorship helps to enhance the credibility of a brand by being associated with a sport or event. ✓ This will help to persuade customers to purchase the business's products or services, as they want to be associated with the brand too. ✓ Sponsorship may therefore result in increased sales and revenues for the business. ✓

(d) Explain **one** method that a business might use to help ensure it provides good customer service. (3)

A business could ensure that its employees have excellent knowledge of the product or service they are selling, ✓ so they can answer any questions and queries a potential customer may ask. ✓ This would result in the customer being able to make a well-informed decision before making a purchase. ✓

137

Set 2 Paper 2 Answers

(e) Discuss the impact to a business of having a hierarchical structure. (6)

One impact is that it may be easier for a line manager or supervisor to check their subordinates' work. This is because in a hierarchical structure, each manager or supervisor has a smaller span of control (compared with those in flat structures), therefore they can work closely with their team to ensure quality, which makes it easier to maintain standards across the organisation.

Another impact is that effective two-way communication is more difficult. This is because there are many layers of management in the organisation for messages to pass through, since channels of communication are long, therefore it is hard for those at the top of the hierarchy to communicate with those lower down. As a result, those lower down may not feel valued or listened to, which may lead to some workers feeling demotivated and working less efficiently.

(Total for Question 3 = 15 marks)
TOTAL FOR SECTION A = 35 MARKS

Writing a good answer

'Discuss' questions will ask you to look at a likely impact, benefit, drawback or similar.

In a 'Discuss' question you should:
- show your **Knowledge and Understanding (AO1)** by giving one or two clear points
- include a minimum of five linked development points across the 1–2 points you have made, to demonstrate your **Analysis (AO3a)**.

A very strong answer because...

✓ **Understanding**: There are two valid points: it is easier for a line manager/supervisor to check their subordinates' work, and effective communication is more difficult. This clearly shows good understanding of the concept.

✓ **Analysis**: There are seven linked strands of development across the two paragraphs, which more than covers the requirement of a minimum of five. There is also good use of connectives, such as 'therefore' and 'this is because', to show these links.

SECTION B
Answer ALL questions.
Read the following extract carefully and then answer Questions 4, 5 and 6.
Write your answers in the spaces provided.

The budget hotel chain *Travelodge* has announced it will be opening six new hotels in the UK. This represents an investment of £45 million in the new hotels, bringing the total number of *Travelodge* hotels in the UK, Ireland and Spain to 595 in 2020. The six new hotels will also create an additional 135 jobs.

In Edinburgh, the new hotel will be a *Travelodge PLUS*, which the company calls its 'budget chic' format. *Travelodge PLUS* hotels include king-size beds, blackout curtains, bespoke wall art and a new-look restaurant. They feature *Travelodge* 'SuperRooms™' which each offer a *Lavazza* coffee machine, hypoallergenic pillows, a three-jet shower and 32" *Samsung Freeview* TV. Following feedback from customers, *Travelodge PLUS* hotels are designed to appeal to budget travellers who want a touch of luxury.

However, the company still has a strong focus on budget to help them compete with rivals such as *Premier Inn*. Rooms are on offer from £29 per night, and dinner deals from £12.25, with special offers for families, such as children eating free.

Travelodge continues to have a strong online presence, receiving more than a million visits a week to its website. It uses appealing discounts to compete with other online sites such as *Booking.com* and *Expedia*.

---

4 (a) Outline **one** drawback to *Travelodge* of being a budget hotel chain. (2)

One drawback is that the profit margin on each sale is very low. ✓ Therefore, Travelodge will have to ensure more rooms are booked in order to break even than if it charged a higher price. ✓

(b) Analyse the benefit to *Travelodge* of launching *Travelodge PLUS*. (6)

Launching Travelodge PLUS will allow the hotel company to differentiate itself from rival firms such as Premier Inn. As a result, Travelodge will be able to attract more travellers who want to stay in the SuperRooms, therefore the hotel company's cash-flow may increase, making it easier to purchase future budget chic hotels.

Although still cheap in comparison to rivals such as Premier Inn, introducing these chic hotels to its portfolio may allow the hotel chain to charge slightly more than it does for its ordinary hotels. This may lead to the hotel business receiving more revenue. This may allow Travelodge to recoup the £45m that has been invested more quickly, allowing the hotel chain to receive a return on its investment in a shorter amount of time.

(Total for Question 4 = 8 marks)

Writing a good answer

In an 'Analyse' question you should:
- clearly **apply your answer to the context** throughout (AO2)
- give one or two clear points and a minimum of five linked development points, to demonstrate your **Analysis (AO3a)**.

A very strong answer because...

✓ **Analysis**: Two valid points are made (differentiating from others and charge slightly more), each with three clear linked strands of development.

✓ **Application**: Application is shown by references to 'hotel company', 'rival firms such as Premier Inn', 'travellers', 'budget chic hotels', and the £45m investment.

---

5 Figure 2 shows information relating to *Travelodge's* revenue for 2018.

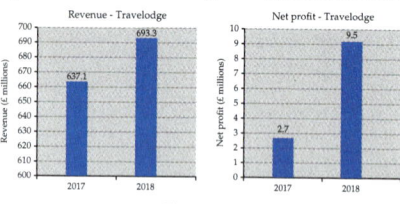

Figure 2
Revenue - Travelodge: 2017 = 637.1, 2018 = 693.3 (£ millions)
Net profit - Travelodge: 2017 = 2.7, 2018 = 9.5 (£ millions)

(Data source: https://www.travelodge.co.uk/sites/default/files/T&L_2018_signed_accounts.pdf)

(a) Using the information in Figure 2, calculate, to two decimal places, the percentage change in *Travelodge's* revenue between 2017 and 2018. You are advised to show your workings. (2)

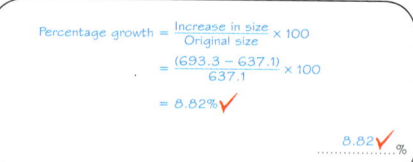

$$\text{Percentage growth} = \frac{\text{Increase in size}}{\text{Original size}} \times 100$$

$$= \frac{(693.3 - 637.1)}{637.1} \times 100$$

$$= 8.82\% ✓$$

8.82 ✓ %

(b) Using the information in Figure 2, calculate, to two decimal places, *Travelodge's* net profit margin in 2018. You are advised to show your workings. (2)

$$\text{Net profit margin (\%)} = \frac{\text{Net profit}}{\text{Sales revenue}} \times 100$$

$$= \frac{9.2m}{693.3m} \times 100 ✓$$

1.33 ✓ %

(c) Analyse the impact on *Travelodge* of selling through its website. (6)

One impact is that there is lots of competition from sites such as Booking.com and Expedia. This would make it harder to attract travellers, therefore the hotel chain must spend money on promoting its website. This increases the fixed costs, which means the company has to have more rooms booked in order to break even.

A second impact is that the travel company would have a larger market of potential travellers to sell to. Tourists like to compare the price of hotels before purchasing, so being online will allow travellers to see the value for money that budget chic hotels offer. Therefore, the hotel chain may have more rooms booked, potentially leading to increased profits.

(Total for Question 5 = 10 marks)

Writing a good answer

In an 'Analyse' question you should:
- clearly **apply your answer to the context** throughout (AO2)
- give one or two clear points and a minimum of five linked development points, to demonstrate your **Analysis (AO3a)**.

A very strong answer because...

✓ **Analysis**: This answer follows the two-paragraph approach. The first paragraph contains a first valid impact (lots of competition online) followed by four linked strands of development. The second paragraph contains a second valid impact (a larger market) with a further three linked strands of development. Therefore, the answer meets the minimum requirement of five linked strands of development for **Analysis**.

✓ **Application**: In both paragraphs, context is used widely, and the response continually links back to the hotel market. The skill of application is fully shown by references to 'Booking.com', 'Expedia', 'travellers', 'rooms', 'budget chic hotels' and 'hotel chain'.

---

6 (a) State **one** piece of market data that *Travelodge* may have considered when deciding whether to build a *Travelodge PLUS* in Edinburgh. (1)

The company should have looked at which other hotel chains already had hotels in this city ✓

(b) Outline **one** reason why it is important that *Travelodge* responds to customer feedback. (2)

It is important so that the hotel company can adapt its hotels to better meet customer needs ✓ This will help lead to increased sales for the hotel chain in the future ✓

138

Set 2 Paper 2 Answers

To finance further *Travelodge PLUS* hotels, *Travelodge* is considering the following two options.

Option 1: Borrow more money from banks.

Option 2: Sell assets.

(c) Justify which **one** of these two options *Travelodge* should choose. (9)

> I believe that Travelodge should finance future hotels by selling assets, as it is a cheaper source of finance than loans (on which the company would have to pay interest). This is important because Travelodge has already invested £45m. Having no additional interest payments would allow Travelodge's costs to remain low, which would enable the hotel chain to charge customers a lower amount for a night's stay when compared with rivals such as Premier Inn, potentially increasing the number of travellers that choose to stay at a Travelodge hotel. This means that the new budget chic hotels may be able to break even more quickly.
>
> However, selling assets, such as older hotels, may be a bad idea, as Travelodge needs these assets in order to provide their overnight stays. If the hotel chain sells older hotels to raise money for Travelodge PLUS hotels, the hotel chain may lose out on potential custom from travellers in certain areas where they are sold. This could mean the travel company loses sales to other hotel chains such as Holiday Inn, who continue to have hotels in those locations. This will harm the hotel chain's cash-flow.
>
> In conclusion selling assets will be the best option. The main reason for this decision is that Travelodge is a budget hotel chain and must do all that it can to keep the price for overnight stays as low as possible, so by selling assets rather than taking out a loan they avoid repaying additional interest. However, this decision will depend on what the assets are that the hotel chains decides to sell. If it sells hotels that are still currently attracting travellers then this may not be the best option as it will need those hotels to provide its service. However, if it has hotels that have made

continual losses, then selling them will not only raise money for the Travelodge PLUS hotels, but prevent Travelodge from making further losses.

(Total for Question 6 = 12 marks)
TOTAL FOR SECTION B = 30 MARKS

Writing a good answer

'Justify' questions will ask you to make a choice between two options. **There is no need to discuss both options.**

When answering a 'Justify' question, aim to write three paragraphs.

- **Paragraph 1:** Select the option you feel is best and state why, using *at least three* linked strands of development to demonstrate **Analysis (AO3a)**. Make sure you refer to the context throughout, to demonstrate **Application (AO2)**.
- **Paragraph 2:** Explain a drawback of the option you have chosen, to show balance and **Evaluation (AO3b)**. Again, include *at least three* linked strands of development to demonstrate **Analysis (AO3a)**, and refer to context to demonstrate **Application (AO2)**. By including three linked strands of development in both paragraphs, you will be more confident that you are covering the overall requirement of five linked strands of development for this answer.
- **Paragraph 3:** Conclude by giving the main reason why you selected your option. Use the 'It depends' rule. This is another way of demonstrating **Evaluation (AO3b)**, and should also refer to the context for **Application (AO2)**.

A very strong answer because...

✓ **Application:** All three paragraphs use context widely – the response is rooted in the case study, with multiple examples of Application in every paragraph.

✓ **Analysis:** The first paragraph contains four linked strands of development required, and the second paragraph also has several linked strands. The response also uses connectives, such as 'because' and 'this could mean...', extremely well.

✓ **Evaluation:** The response is balanced: a benefit and a drawback of Option 2. There is a substantial conclusion that explores the main reason why Option 2 is better, but there is also consideration of what the decision depends on as the answer suggests that the decision depends on what assets they actually sell.

SECTION C
Answer ALL questions.
Read the following extract carefully and then answer Question 7.
Write your answers in the spaces provided.

Primark is a fashion retailer that offers a varied range of products, including children's clothing, men's wear, women's wear, homeware, accessories, beauty products and confectionery. *Primark* now has over 350 stores in 11 countries across Europe and America.

One country *Primark* operates in is bargain-hunting Germany, where it plans to open two more stores in the next year as part of its growth strategy. This move abroad has been successful for *Primark*, as German shoppers favour good quality at a low price, something that has become synonymous with *Primark*.

Primark has also recognised the need to improve its ethical stance and as such has emphasised its commitment to environmental standards and safer working conditions, as it fights for market share. German customers demand high ethical standards and the retailer has started to display 'Primark Cares' posters in its German stores. These contain information about its factories and how it sources raw materials. As *Primark* does not manufacture its own products, it must be very selective about the factories it works with to maintain both quality for its customers and decent working conditions and wages for the factory workers. It achieves this by requiring every supplier to agree to achieving internationally-recognised standards, which it sets out in the *Primark* Code of Conduct. In addition, each factory is audited by an Ethical Trade and Environmental Sustainability Team, which comprises more than 100 experts who are based in key sourcing countries and who monitor compliance against *Primark's* Code. This procurement is key to *Primark's* success.

Primark faces strong competition from another discount retailer, *H&M*. Recently *Primark* has been successful in drawing customers away from its Swedish rivals. However, *H&M* is also putting a bigger emphasis on sustainability. As concerns about environmental impact are increasingly at the front of customers' minds, both *H&M* and *Primark* are promoting recycling and improved cotton-farming methods.

(References: https://www.businessoffashion.com/articles/news-analysis/primark-sharpens-ethical-focus-in-fight-for-market-share and https://www.primark.com/en/our-ethics/newsroom/2018/primark-expands-sustainable-cotton-programme-into-second-major-sourcing-country)

---

7 (a) Define the term procurement. (1)

> Obtaining the right supplies from the right supplier. ✓

Figure 3 shows the market share of major clothing retailers in the UK in 2008 and 2018.

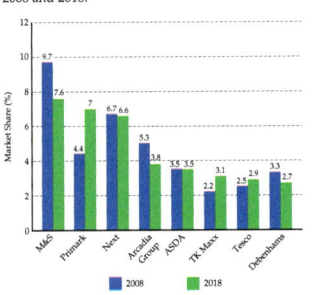

Figure 3
(Adapted from: https://www.just-style.com/news/ms-perilously-close-to-losing-top-clothing-retailer-spot_id133576.aspx)

(b) Using Figure 3, identify the retailer that achieved the greatest increase in market share between 2008 and 2018. (1)

> Primark ✓

(c) Outline **one** reason why *Primark* has chosen to open stores in Germany. (2)

> Primark has chosen Germany, as the customers there like to have low prices for products. ✓ This has led to Primark increasing its sales, as it is known for selling affordable fashion. ✓

To improve its competitiveness against other fashion retailers, *Primark* is considering the following two options.

Option 1: Concentrate on keeping prices lower than competitors.

Option 2: Improve its ethical standards.

(d) Justify which **one** of these two options *Primark* should choose. (9)

> Option 2 is the most appropriate to improve competitiveness, because by focusing on ethical standards, Primark will improve its reputation in the clothing market. Customers feel good about purchasing T-shirts made from ethically-sourced cotton, so by selling such items, Primark will continue to attract customers away from rivals such as H&M. Should this happen, Primark's sales will increase, which may lead to the company's revenue and profits increasing, so improving the clothing firm's competitiveness.
>
> However, focusing more on ethical standards could be more expensive for the company, as it may involve paying higher variable costs to suppliers who meet the internationally recognised standards as set out in the Primark Code of Conduct. This could lead to Primark having to increase the price of its clothes, which could result in the company becoming less competitive against rivals such as H&M, and may result in falling sales and profits, as well as Primark failing to expand into new markets such as Germany.
>
> In conclusion, I believe that focusing more on ethical standards is the best option for Primark, as it is vital in today's world for clothing retailers to behave responsibly. One reason for this is, with the rise in social media, anyone could report a company such as Primark for unethical practice in terms of where it buys its clothes, and this could have an incredibly damaging impact on the company's brand and therefore its competitiveness. However, my decision depends on how ethically minded Primark's customers are: if customers do not care where the T-shirts are sourced

139

Set 2 Paper 2 Answers

from then concentrating on keeping costs, and therefore prices, low could be more important to increasing Primark's competitiveness against other fashion retailers.

Writing a good answer

'Justify' questions will ask you to make a choice between two options. **There is no need to discuss both options.**

When answering a 'Justify' question, aim to write three paragraphs.

- Paragraph 1: Select the option you feel is best and state why, using at least three linked strands of development to demonstrate **Analysis (AO3a)**. Make sure you refer to the context throughout, to demonstrate **Application (AO2)**.
- Paragraph 2: Explain a drawback of the option you have chosen, to show balance and **Evaluation (AO3b)**. Again, include at least three linked strands of development to demonstrate **Analysis (AO3a)**, and refer to **context** to demonstrate **Application (AO2)**.

By including three linked strands of development in both paragraphs, you can be more confident that you are covering the overall requirement of five linked strands of development for this answer.

- Paragraph 3: Conclude by giving the main reason why you selected your option. Use the 'It depends' rule. This is another way of demonstrating **Evaluation (AO3b)**, and should also refer to the **context** for **Application (AO2)**.

A very strong answer because...

✓ **Application**: There are various references to the case study throughout; for example, 'clothing market', 'T-Shirts made from ethically sourced cotton', '*H&M*', '*Primark* Code of Conduct', 'clothes', 'expand into new markets such as Germany' and 'clothing retailers'.

✓ **Analysis**: There are two valid points, which are together supported by more than five linked development points across the two paragraphs.

✓ **Evaluation**: A balanced response is given, as a benefit and drawback of Option 2 have been considered. In the conclusion the student supports their argument by looking at what is 'vital' to *Primark*, but also considers that the decision ultimately depends on the perspective of *Primark*'s customers.

(e) Evaluate whether *Primark's* relationship with its suppliers is the key factor in determining the profitability of the business. You should use the information provided as well as your knowledge of business. (12)

One reason why Primark's relationship with its suppliers is key is because the supplier is responsible for the quality of the clothes Primark has to sell. Primark does not own its own factories so cannot alter the quality of the fashion items it sells. If the suppliers Primark use produce T-shirts that are not as good quality as those sold by rival fashion retailers, then Primark may fail to meet its customers' needs. This could cause Primark to lose sales, if customers decide to buy better quality clothes from companies such as H&M, ultimately leading to a fall in Primark's profitability. However, it may be that quality isn't key to Primark's profitability, but whether its growth strategy of moving into foreign markets continues to be successful. The case study mentions that Primark plans to open two new stores in Germany: this is a very expensive process, as Primark has to purchase the stores, hire staff and undertake marketing activities so that it can establish itself as a prominent fashion retailer in these new locations. If Primark fails to achieve sufficient sales in order to break even, then the company would not be profitable and could experience financial losses. In conclusion, there are several factors that will determine whether Primark is profitable; the fashion retailer's relationship with suppliers is just one factor that is important. Primark must have good quality fashion supplies at reasonable prices, delivered when required. It also needs its customers to buy sufficient clothes to cover the costs of supplies, so marketing is important too. Therefore, the fashion retailer's success is dependent on a combination of factors; if any one of them is not addressed properly,

Primark will not be profitable and will lose its competitiveness in the fashion industry.

(Total for Question 7 = 25 marks)
TOTAL FOR SECTION C = 25 MARKS
TOTAL FOR PAPER = 90 MARKS

Writing a good answer

In an 'Evaluate' question you should aim for three paragraphs.

- Paragraph 1: Show your **Knowledge and Understanding (AO1)**; for example, give a definition of one of the key terms. You should also use Business terms throughout. Then provide arguments in support of the statement, with at least three linked development points to show thorough **Analysis (AO3a)**. Apply your points to the context throughout **(AO2)**.
- Paragraph 2: Give alternative arguments, with at least three linked development points to show thorough **Analysis (AO3a)**. Apply your points to the context throughout **(AO2)**.

By including three linked strands of development in both paragraphs, you can be more confident that you are covering the overall requirement of five linked strands of development for this answer.

- Paragraph 3: Give a balanced conclusion to demonstrate your **Evaluation (AO3b)**, making use of the 'It depends' argument.

A very strong answer because...

✓ **Understanding**: The Knowledge and Understanding shown is excellent. The answer clearly demonstrates why a relationship with suppliers is important. Good terminology and business theory are used throughout.

✓ **Application**: The answer has referred to context extensively in all three paragraphs and is specific to *Primark* and the clothing industry.

✓ **Analysis**: The first and second paragraphs each contain at least three linked strands of development. The answer therefore achieves the minimum of five linked strands of development across the two points.

✓ **Evaluation**: This is a balanced argument, which states why the relationship with suppliers is key and also suggests why an alternative factor may be more crucial. The conclusion answers the question well, arguing that success is not just down to one individual factor but is the result of a combination of factors.

140

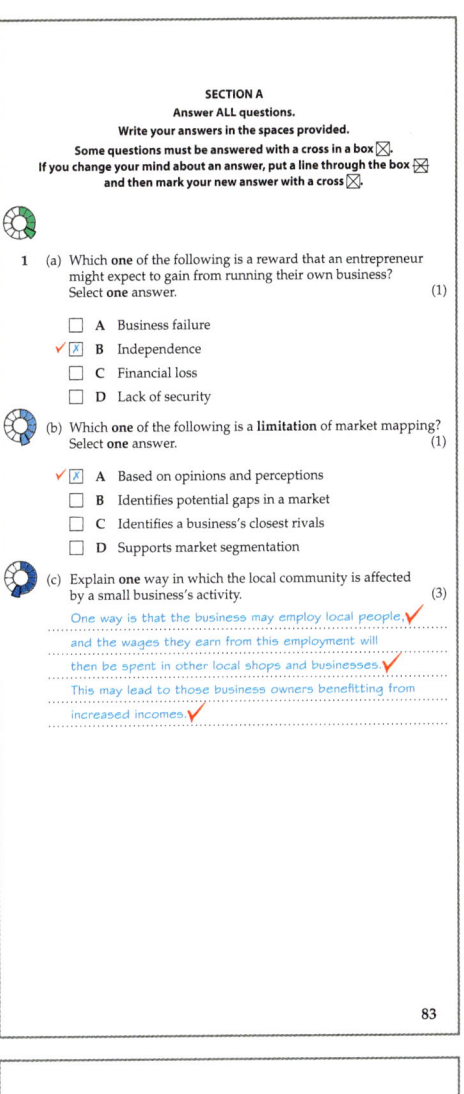

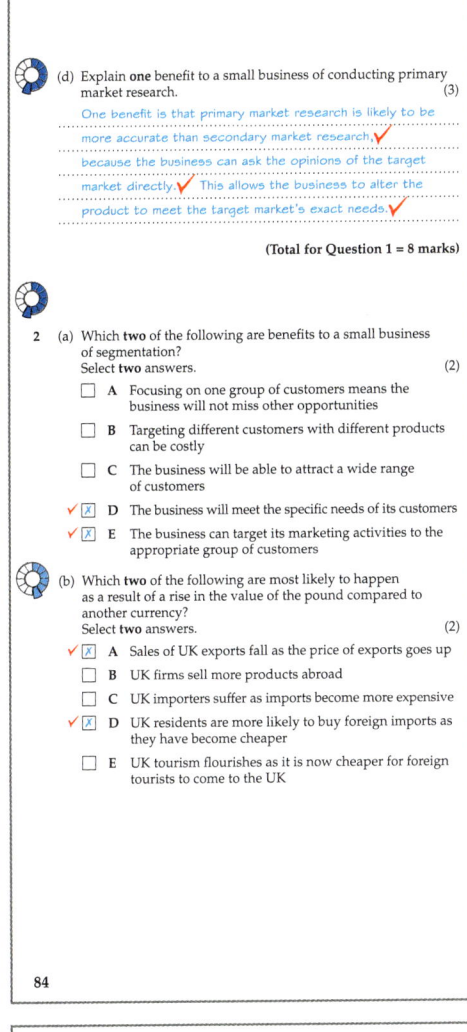

Set 3 Paper 1 Answers

SECTION A
Answer ALL questions.
Write your answers in the spaces provided.
Some questions must be answered with a cross in a box ☒.
If you change your mind about an answer, put a line through the box ☒ and then mark your new answer with a cross ☒.

1 (a) Which **one** of the following is a reward that an entrepreneur might expect to gain from running their own business?
Select **one** answer. (1)

- ☐ A Business failure
- ☒ B Independence ✓
- ☐ C Financial loss
- ☐ D Lack of security

(b) Which **one** of the following is a **limitation** of market mapping?
Select **one** answer. (1)

- ☒ A Based on opinions and perceptions ✓
- ☐ B Identifies potential gaps in a market
- ☐ C Identifies a business's closest rivals
- ☐ D Supports market segmentation

(c) Explain **one** way in which the local community is affected by a small business's activity. (3)

One way is that the business may employ local people, ✓ and the wages they earn from this employment will then be spent in other local shops and businesses. ✓ This may lead to those business owners benefitting from increased incomes. ✓

(d) Explain **one** benefit to a small business of conducting primary market research. (3)

One benefit is that primary market research is likely to be more accurate than secondary market research, ✓ because the business can ask the opinions of the target market directly. ✓ This allows the business to alter the product to meet the target market's exact needs. ✓

(Total for Question 1 = 8 marks)

2 (a) Which **two** of the following are benefits to a small business of segmentation?
Select **two** answers. (2)

- ☐ A Focusing on one group of customers means the business will not miss other opportunities
- ☐ B Targeting different customers with different products can be costly
- ☐ C The business will be able to attract a wide range of customers
- ☒ D The business will meet the specific needs of its customers ✓
- ☒ E The business can target its marketing activities to the appropriate group of customers ✓

(b) Which **two** of the following are most likely to happen as a result of a rise in the value of the pound compared to another currency?
Select **two** answers. (2)

- ☒ A Sales of UK exports fall as the price of exports goes up ✓
- ☐ B UK firms sell more products abroad
- ☐ C UK importers suffer as imports become more expensive
- ☒ D UK residents are more likely to buy foreign imports as they have become cheaper ✓
- ☐ E UK tourism flourishes as it is now cheaper for foreign tourists to come to the UK

Table 1 shows some financial information about a small business.

Selling price (£)	7.50
Fixed costs per year (£)	10 000
Variable cost per unit (£)	2.50
Number of units sold per year	15 000

Table 1

(c) Using the information in Table 1, calculate the number of units the small business needs to sell each year in order to break even. You are advised to show your workings. (2)

$$\text{Break-even point in units} = \frac{\text{Fixed cost}}{(\text{Sales price} - \text{Variable cost})}$$

$$= \frac{10\,000}{(£7.50 - £2.50)} = \frac{10\,000}{£5.00} ✓$$

$$= 2\,000 ✓ \text{ units}$$

(d) Explain **one** way in which a small business can use technology to gain competitive advantage. (3)

A small business could use e-commerce. ✓ This would involve a business selling its goods or services via the internet rather than, or in addition to, a physical store. ✓ Selling in this way may lead to the business being able to reach a wider pool of potential customers. ✓

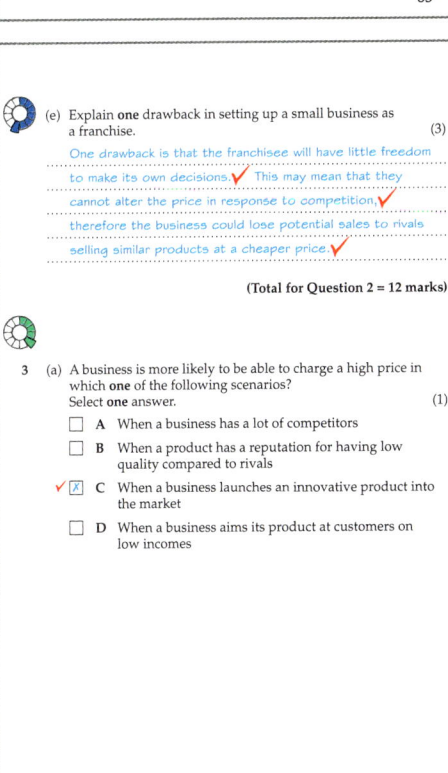

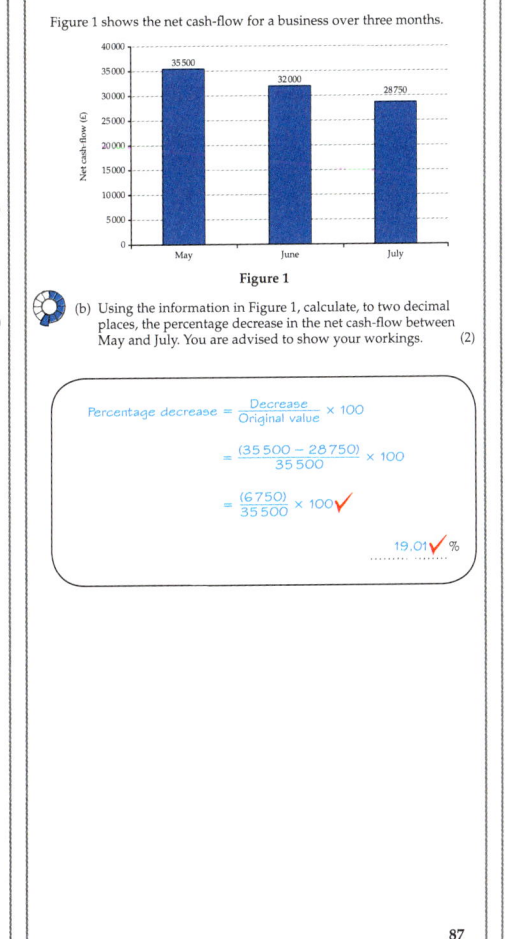

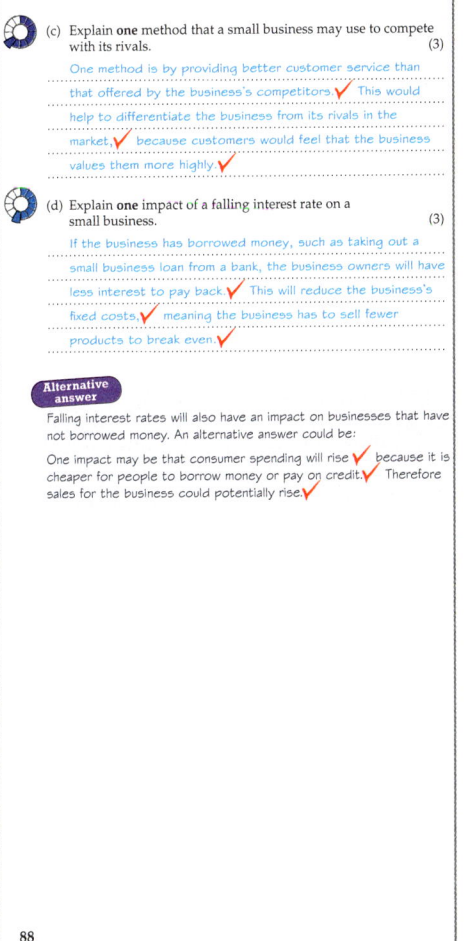

(e) Explain **one** drawback in setting up a small business as a franchise. (3)

One drawback is that the franchisee will have little freedom to make its own decisions. ✓ This may mean that they cannot alter the price in response to competition, ✓ therefore the business could lose potential sales to rivals selling similar products at a cheaper price. ✓

(Total for Question 2 = 12 marks)

3 (a) A business is more likely to be able to charge a high price in which **one** of the following scenarios?
Select **one** answer. (1)

- ☐ A When a business has a lot of competitors
- ☐ B When a product has a reputation for having low quality compared to rivals
- ☒ C When a business launches an innovative product into the market ✓
- ☐ D When a business aims its product at customers on low incomes

Figure 1 shows the net cash-flow for a business over three months.

[Bar chart: May 35 500, June 32 000, July 28 750]

Figure 1

(b) Using the information in Figure 1, calculate, to two decimal places, the percentage decrease in the net cash-flow between May and July. You are advised to show your workings. (2)

$$\text{Percentage decrease} = \frac{\text{Decrease}}{\text{Original value}} \times 100$$

$$= \frac{(35\,500 - 28\,750)}{35\,500} \times 100$$

$$= \frac{(6\,750)}{35\,500} \times 100 ✓$$

$$= 19.01 ✓ \%$$

(c) Explain **one** method that a small business may use to compete with its rivals. (3)

One method is by providing better customer service than that offered by the business's competitors. ✓ This would help to differentiate the business from its rivals in the market, ✓ because customers would feel that the business values them more highly. ✓

(d) Explain **one** impact of a falling interest rate on a small business. (3)

If the business has borrowed money, such as taking out a small business loan from a bank, the business owners will have less interest to pay back. ✓ This will reduce the business's fixed costs, ✓ meaning the business has to sell fewer products to break even. ✓

Alternative answer

Falling interest rates will also have an impact on businesses that have not borrowed money. An alternative answer could be:

One impact may be that consumer spending will rise ✓ because it is cheaper for people to borrow money or pay on credit. ✓ Therefore sales for the business could potentially rise. ✓

141

Set 3 Paper 1 Answers

(e) Discuss the reason why cash is important to a small business. (6)

> Cash is important because without it the business may be unable to pay wages to its employees. This will hugely demotivate the employees, who may cease working. This could result in the business not being able to serve its customers who, as a result, may decide to go to a rival business.
>
> Cash is also important because if there is no cash the business will not be able to pay for advertising. This would mean that potential customers might be unaware of the business's existence and product offering. This could lead to insufficient sales for the business to cover its costs, which may result in the business failing.

(Total for Question 3 = 15 marks)
TOTAL FOR SECTION A = 35 MARKS

Writing a good answer

'Discuss' questions will ask you to look at a likely impact, benefit, drawback or similar. In a 'Discuss' question you should:
- show your **Knowledge and Understanding (AO1)** by giving one or two clear points
- include a minimum of five linked development points across the 1–2 points you have made, to demonstrate your **Analysis (AO3a)**.

A very strong answer because...

✓ **Understanding**: This response clearly demonstrates excellent understanding of business concepts and makes two valid points (cash is important to pay wages and market the business).

✓ **Analysis**: Both paragraphs contain three linked strands of development following on from a valid point, which more than covers the requirement for a minimum of five linked development strands to achieve good marks for **Analysis**.

SECTION B
Answer ALL questions
Read the following extract carefully and then answer Questions 4, 5 and 6. Write your answers in the spaces provided.

Green Cars Ltd is an independent garage that offers car repairs and servicing. It is a family-run business (managed by Frank and his daughter, Megan) and has been trading for over 17 years. Throughout the years, *Green Cars Ltd* has retained its philosophy of traditional values, offering a personal, family service and affordable prices. The company is known for providing a high level of customer service.

After completing some market research, which included the creation of a market map, *Green Cars Ltd* decided to add a car sales division. This would involve purchasing second-hand cars it would then sell on. In order to do this, it needed to borrow money from the bank. Frank and Megan therefore put together a business plan, in order to convince the bank to lend them the money. While the bank manager agreed to the loan, she expressed concern that the current downturn in the economy could cause a drop in car sales, which would negatively affect the success of the new car sales division.

When *Green Cars Ltd* opened 17 years ago, it chose to locate in a small industrial estate on the outskirts of Chedgrave, a small village 10 miles southeast of Norwich. The owners are now considering whether a move to a location closer to a larger town, Beccles, would be more beneficial to the business now that the company is selling cars as well as repairing them. A site has become available in the centre of the town, but the rent for the site at Beccles is much higher than the current rent.

---

4 (a) Outline **one** drawback to *Green Cars Ltd* of being a private limited company. (2)

> One drawback is that Frank and Megan may not agree on decisions to be made. ✓ This may mean that decisions are not made and the garage misses out on business opportunities. ✓

(b) Analyse the impact on *Green Cars Ltd* of borrowing money from the bank to fund the car sales division of the business. (6)

> One impact is that the loan for the purchase of vehicles will be paid back with interest, which will lead to an increase in the fixed costs of the garage. This will mean that Frank and Megan see an increase in the garage's total costs. As a result, the second-hand-car shop will have to sell and repair more vehicles in order to break even. This would then lower the margin of safety for the second-hand-car business, which therefore leads to increased risk of failure.

(Total for Question 4 = 8 marks)

Writing a good answer

'Analyse' questions will ask you to look at an impact, advantage, drawback or similar. In an 'Analyse' question you should:
- clearly **apply** your answer to the **context** throughout (AO2)
- give **one or two clear points** and a minimum of **five linked development points**, to demonstrate your **Analysis (AO3a)**.

A very strong answer because...

✓ **Application**: Context is used throughout this answer, which includes references to 'purchase of vehicles', 'garage', the owners 'Frank and Megan' and 'sell and repair more vehicles'.

✓ **Analysis**: This response provides a valid point (the loan needs to be paid back with interest) followed by five clear and logical linked strands of development, signposted with connectives.

---

5 In order to purchase second-hand cars for its new car sales division, *Green Cars Ltd* borrowed £125 000. It will repay the loan over 10 years. The interest rate the bank charges is 5 per cent per year.

(a) Calculate the total amount of money that will be repaid by *Green Cars Ltd* to the bank during the lifetime of the loan. You are advised to show your workings. (2)

> Annual interest rate = Loan amount × percentage rate
> = £125 000 × 0.05 = £6 250
>
> Total interest = Annual interest × number of years
> = 6 250 × 10 years
> = £62 500
>
> Total repaid = 125 000 + 62 500 ✓
> = £187 500
>
> £ 187 500 ✓

Table 2 shows the projected cash-flow information for *Green Cars Ltd* after taking out the bank loan.

Receipts	£275 000
Payment for fixed costs	£56 000
Payment for variable costs	£123 675

Table 2

(b) Calculate the net cash-flow for *Green Cars Ltd*, based on the information shown in Table 2. You are advised to show your workings. (2)

> Net cash-flow = cash inflow − cash outflow
> Cash inflow = £275 000
>
> Cash outflow = 56 000
> + 123 675
> 179 675
>
> Net cash-flow = 275 000
> − 179 675
> 95 325
>
> £ 95 325 ✓

(c) Analyse the drawback that an economic downturn may have on *Green Cars Ltd*. (6)

> An economic downturn may cause more unemployment, which would mean that motorists have less disposable income as a result of the increasing unemployment in the economy. This may lead to customers being more reluctant to make big purchases such as buying a vehicle, which could lead to fewer sales for the second-hand-car sales division. This would mean the garage's revenue could fall and therefore Frank and Megan would see a fall in profits if the car business's costs stay the same. If this situation continues it could threaten the garage's survival.

(Total for Question 5 = 10 marks)

Writing a good answer

'Analyse' questions will ask you to look at an impact, advantage, drawback or similar. In an 'Analyse' question you should:
- clearly **apply** your answer to the **context** throughout your answer (AO2)
- give **one or two clear points** and a minimum of **five linked development points**, to demonstrate your **Analysis (AO3a)**.

A very strong answer because...

✓ **Application**: Context is used throughout. There are multiple references to *Green Cars Ltd* as a car repair and sales business, including 'motorists', 'vehicle', 'second-hand-car sales division' and 'garage', as well as referring to the owners, 'Frank and Megan'.

✓ **Analysis**: This paragraph makes a valid point (motorists may have less income as a result of increasing unemployment), which is then supported by five linked strands of development. The answer makes good use of connectives such as 'this may lead to', 'this would mean' and 'therefore' to show these links.

---

6 (a) State **one** reason why *Green Cars Ltd* decided to create a business plan. (1)

> To get a bank loan so the car business could purchase second-hand cars to sell on. ✓

(b) Outline **one** benefit to Frank and Megan of *Green Cars Ltd* conducting primary research. (2)

> One benefit is that they can find out if there are any rival garages in the local area. ✓ This will help them to spot if there is a gap in the market. ✓

142

Green Cars Ltd is considering two options with regards to its location, in order to try and improve future profitability.

Option 1: Remain in its current location on the industrial estate, where it has always been.

Option 2: Move to the new premises in the larger town of Beccles.

(c) Justify which **one** of these two options *Green Cars Ltd* should choose. (9)

> I believe Green Cars Ltd should relocate its garage and car sales business to the larger town of Beccles. This is because the car business will be closer to a larger pool of customers with motoring needs, as the site is located in the centre of the town. Therefore, more people will notice the garage and be inclined to use it when they need a repair or to purchase a vehicle. This will lead to more customers wanting a repair service or purchasing a car, which may increase Frank and Megan's revenue, potentially increasing their profits.
>
> However, changing potentially to the larger town of Beccles will cost more. Not only will Frank and Megan have to pay the costs of relocation, the rent on the new premises will be a lot more than what they are currently paying. This will increase fixed costs for the garage business, causing Green Cars Ltd's total costs to increase, which could potentially lead to lower profit for the car business if sales do not increase.
>
> Overall, I believe that moving to the town of Beccles is the best option. As Frank and Megan have recently introduced the second-hand-car sales division to their business, it is vital that people are aware that they now have vehicles for sale as well as offering car repairs and services. Moving to a more populated area will allow this to happen. However, whether it actually leads to an improvement in future profitability will depend on whether Frank and Megan can attract sufficient customers so that the increase in revenue will be greater than the increased costs they experience as a result of the relocation.

(Total for Question 6 = 12 marks)
TOTAL FOR SECTION B = 30 MARKS

Writing a good answer

'Justify' questions will ask you to make a choice between two options. **There is no need to discuss both options.** When answering a 'Justify' question, aim to write three paragraphs.

- **Paragraph 1:** Select the option you feel is best and state why, using at least three **linked strands of development** to demonstrate **Analysis (AO3a)**. Make sure you refer to the **context** throughout, to demonstrate **Application (AO2)**.
- **Paragraph 2:** Explain a drawback of the option you have chosen, to show balance and **Evaluation (AO3b)**. Again, include at least three **linked strands of development** to demonstrate **Analysis (AO3a)**, and refer to **context** to demonstrate **Application (AO2)**.
  By including three linked strands of development in both paragraphs, you can be more confident that you are covering the overall requirement of five linked strands of development for this answer.
- **Paragraph 3:** Conclude by giving the main reason why you selected your option. Use the 'It depends' rule. This is another way of demonstrating **Evaluation (AO3b)**, and should also refer to the context for **Application (AO2)**.

A very strong answer because...

✓ **Application:** The answer refers to the case study throughout, for example stating that the town of Beccles is more populated and the rent of the new location will be higher. Constant reference is made to the garage and car sales business.

✓ **Analysis:** There are at least eight linked strands of development across the first two paragraphs, clearly shown by the effective use of connectives, which more than covers the requirement of five linked strands of development for Analysis.

✓ **Evaluation:** The answer concludes with a balanced argument that considers the benefit and drawback of the change in location. There is a clear statement of the main reason why Option 2 has been chosen as well as effective use of the 'It depends' rule.

Set 3 Paper 1 Answers

SECTION C
Answer ALL questions.
Read the following extract carefully and then answer Question 7.
Write your answers in the spaces provided.

Baker's Dozen is a delicatessen shop and café serving homemade cooking, baking, specialities and freshly brewed coffee. It is a small business in the centre of the South Norfolk village of Loddon. The village is popular with tourists holidaying by boat on the nearby Norfolk Broads. In the village there are two other cafés – *Toffee Cake* (a rival upmarket café) and *Tim's Teas* (a more affordable option), both of which also target the tourist trade.

Baker's Dozen was set up as a partnership by three local women – Ashanti, Jo and Helen. The partners all want to bring a fresh style of café to the area by offering high quality, locally sourced produce. The women believe they have found a gap in the market, as there is no other local café with a deli shop (where people can buy food and drink to take home), but they didn't carry out any formal market research to determine this.

The café sells handmade pastries, sandwiches and cakes, all of which are made on the premises by the partners, who use high quality, locally sourced ingredients. The deli shop sells local cheeses, Italian meats and antipasti, as well as the more traditional pastries and cakes.

The partners decided the quality of the food and produce they sell should be reflected in the prices they charge. By the end of their first year of trading, they hadn't quite made the profit they had set themselves as an objective, so they decided to review the sales figures for both the café and the deli shop. In the café, the average spend by the 3750 customers they had that year was £12.00. The cost of making the food and drink they served them amounted to £5.50 and fixed costs for the café were £15 000.

---

7 (a) State **one** impact that legislation may have on *Baker's Dozen*. (1)

> The kitchen where the food is prepared must meet health and safety requirements. ✓

(b) Using the information contained in the case study, calculate *Baker's Dozen's* total costs for the year. You are advised to show your workings. (2)

> Fixed costs = £15 000   Total costs = Fixed costs + Variable costs
>
> Variable costs = 3750   = £15 000
>   × £5.50   + £20 625
>   £20 625   £35 625 ✓
>
>   £35 625 ✓

(c) State **one** way in which *Baker's Dozen* has added value to the food it sells in the café. (1)

> One way is that the food sold at the deli café is made using only locally sourced ingredients. ✓

To make *Baker's Dozen* more competitive against its local rivals, the owners are considering the following two options.

Option 1: Charge lower prices in the deli counter and café sections, to be more comparable to competitors.

Option 2: Develop the deli counter further by providing a wider range of products.

(d) Justify which **one** of these two options *Baker's Dozen* should choose. (9)

> I think that Ashanti, Jo and Helen should choose to develop the deli counter further. This is because the deli makes their café unique compared to their rivals Toffee Cake and Tim's Teas. These other businesses are simply cafés and do not provide the opportunity for shoppers to buy food and drink to take home. Therefore, by being unique, Ashanti, Jo and Helen's deli café will appeal to many of the tourists visiting the area as providing a special experience, which will potentially lead to more sales for both sections of their business, as people may come for a cup of coffee while also buying food and drink to take home.
>
> However, to increase the range of food and drink sold may be expensive because Ashanti, Jo and Helen will have to hold a large amount of different fresh products, as customers will be disappointed if they don't stock what they need. This will increase Ashanti, Jo and Helen's cash outflows, as they will need to pay for the food before they sell it in their delicatessen. This could lead to them being less competitive as they have a greater financial outlay.
>
> In conclusion, whether developing the deli counter further will make the food and drink business more competitive depends on the need for this from customers, so Ashanti, Jo and Helen should conduct some market research prior to going ahead. However, to be competitive, it is vital that the deli café is unique, and if they were simply to lower prices then they would be competing with Tim's only on price. Therefore, offering an upmarket farm-shop-style deli, as well as a place to sit and consume refreshments, will help Baker's Dozen to stand out from the local café-only competitors.

Writing a good answer

'Justify' questions will ask you to make a choice between two options. **There is no need to discuss both options.**

When answering a 'Justify' question, aim to write three paragraphs.

- **Paragraph 1:** Select the option you feel is best and state why, using at least three linked strands of development to demonstrate **Analysis (AO3a)**. Make sure you refer to the context throughout, to demonstrate **Application (AO2)**.
- **Paragraph 2:** Explain a drawback of the option you have chosen, to show balance and **Evaluation (AO3b)**. Again, include at least three linked strands of development to demonstrate **Analysis (AO3a)**, and refer to context to demonstrate **Application (AO2)**.
  By including three linked strands of development in both paragraphs, you can be more confident that you are covering the overall requirement of five linked strands of development for this answer.
- **Paragraph 3:** Conclude by giving the main reason why you selected your option. Use the 'It depends' rule. This is another way of demonstrating **Evaluation (AO3b)**, and should also refer to the context for **Application (AO2)**.

A very strong answer because...

✓ **Application:** There is clear and continuous use of context throughout the response; for example, references are made to food and drink, the owners Ashanti, Jo and Helen, and local competitors.

✓ **Analysis:** Across both paragraphs there is more than the minimum of five linked strands of development. The use of connectives such as 'this could lead to', 'this is because', 'therefore' and 'however' clearly demonstrates this skill.

✓ **Evaluation:** There is a balanced consideration of the advantages and disadvantages of Option 2. The answer also acknowledges that *Baker's Dozen* success is not guaranteed and explores how the business's competitiveness depends on it being 'unique'.

143

Set 3 Paper 1 Answers

(e) Evaluate whether the lack of detailed market research was the main reason why the owners of *Baker's Dozen* did not make as much profit as they expected. You should use the information provided as well as your knowledge of business. (12)

Market research is the process of gathering information about the market and customers' needs and wants in order to help inform business decisions. Lack of market research can be blamed for the small business not making as much profit as anticipated, because Ashanti, Jo and Helen failed to fully appreciate the level of competition the other cafés would provide. The fact that Toffee Cake and Tim's Teas were already well established and aiming at the tourist trade meant there was strong competition for customers. This could have led to the café not receiving as many sales as anticipated, which may have contributed to the café and deli shop only making £9375 profit in its first year. Had Ashanti, Jo and Helen conducted thorough market research they may have realised how competitive the café market in Loddon is. However, you could argue that the lack of success was down to poor promotion of the café and deli. Despite the lack of market research, Ashanti, Jo and Helen have a unique concept compared to their rivals, Toffee Cake and Tim's Teas. They have a delicatessen counter whereas the other cafés do not. Perhaps if the owners had promoted this side of the business more, more people would know that Baker's Dozen also sells local cheeses, Italian meats, antipasti and cakes, as well as being a café. Better promotion, such as advertising around the Norfolk Broads, could mean that the deli café gets more customers, and as a result makes more revenue and therefore more profit – though this depends on the amount spent on promotion.

Overall, I believe that lack of market research was the main contributor to Ashanti, Jo and Helen not making as much profit as they had anticipated. To be successful in business, it is crucial that you sell something that customers need and want, and Ashanti, Jo and Helen never found out whether there was a need for a café and delicatessen in Loddon.

However, success is not dependent on market research alone, and therefore other factors – such as a lack of promotion – may also have contributed to the Baker's Dozen café and deli not meeting its profit targets.

(Total for Question 7 = 25 marks)
TOTAL FOR SECTION C = 25 MARKS
TOTAL FOR PAPER = 90 MARKS

Writing a good answer

When answering an 'Evaluate' question, aim for three paragraphs.

- **Paragraph 1:** Show your **Knowledge and Understanding (AO1)**; for example, give a definition of one of the key terms. You should also use Business terms throughout. Then provide arguments in support of the statement, with at least three linked development points to show thorough **Analysis (AO3a)**. **Use the context throughout (AO2)**.
- **Paragraph 2:** Give alternative arguments, with at least three linked development points to show thorough **Analysis (AO3a)**. **Apply your points to the context** throughout **(AO2)**.

By including three linked strands of development in both paragraphs, you can be more confident that you are covering the overall requirement of five linked strands of development for this answer.

- **Paragraph 3:** Give a balanced conclusion to demonstrate your **Evaluation (AO3b)**, making use of the 'It depends' argument.

A very strong answer because…

✓ **Understanding:** The student starts their answer with a clear definition of market research. They use business terminology accurately and explain business concepts well.

✓ **Application:** Excellent reference is made to the case study throughout. For example, the student highlights the level of competition between cafés in Loddon and the impact of tourism in Norfolk, as well as giving an accurate figure for the amount of profit *Baker's Dozen* made in its first year.

✓ **Analysis:** The student has included more than five linked strands of development across both paragraphs, and uses connectives well to make these links clear.

✓ **Evaluation:** The student has provided a balanced response, suggesting why market research may be the key factor behind *Baker's Dozen* low profits as well as giving an alternative argument for this (lack of promotion). The conclusion clearly justifies which argument is seen as stronger while also recognising that it is difficult to discount other factors completely.

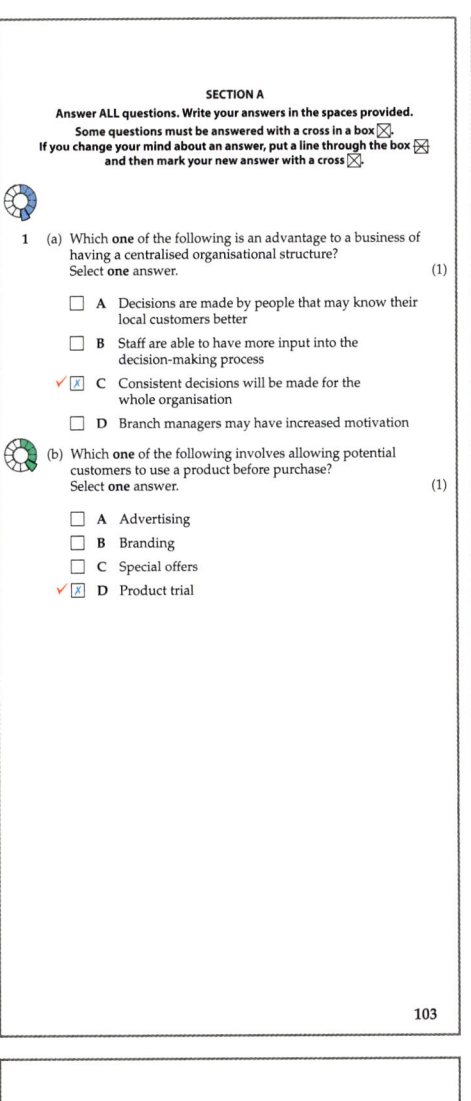

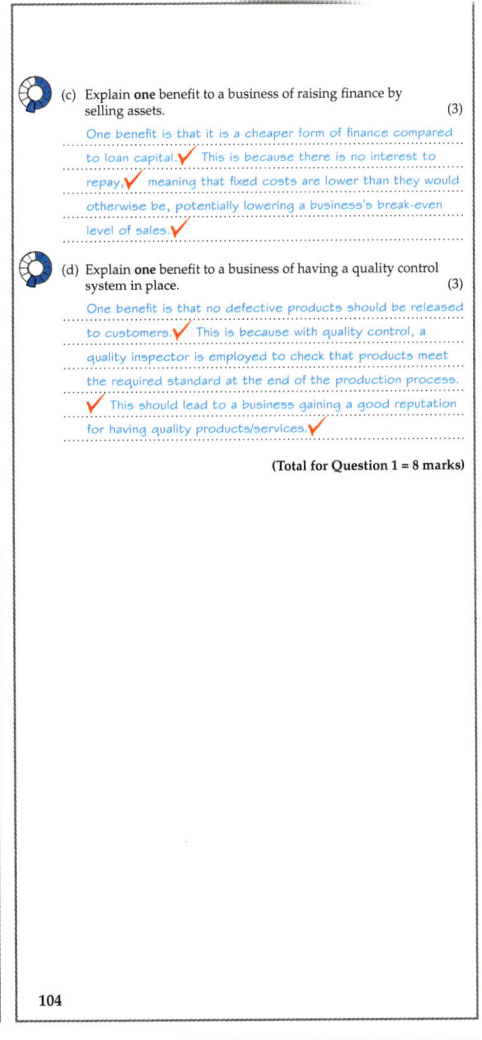

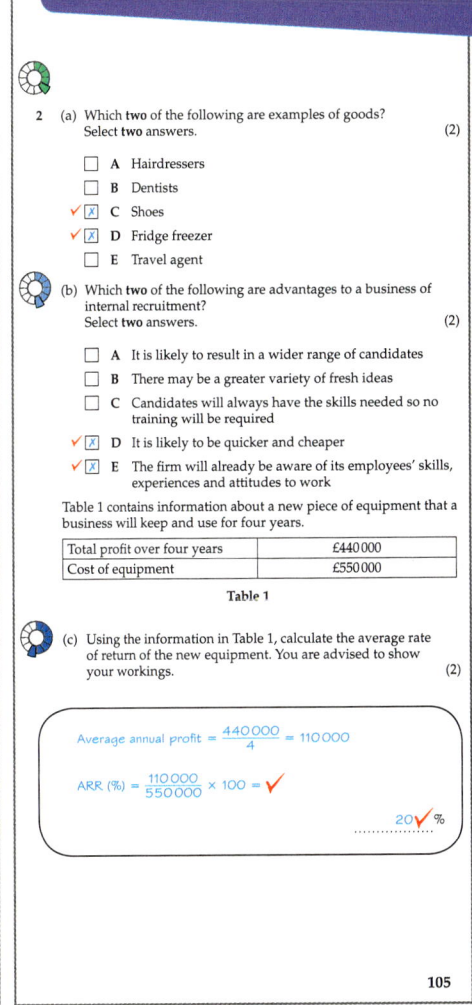

Set 3 Paper 2 Answers

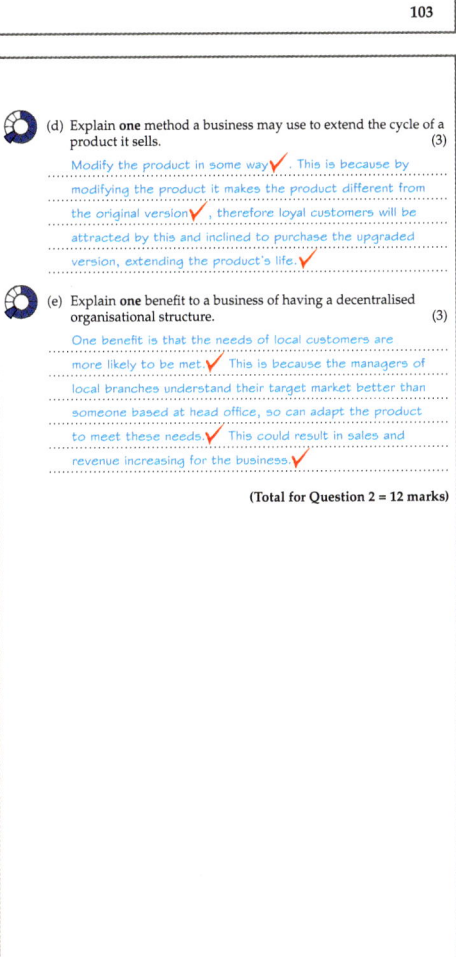

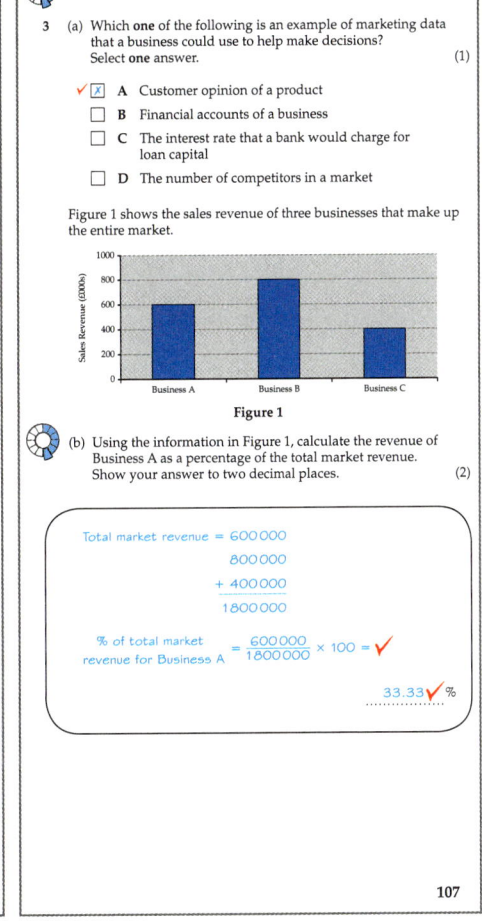

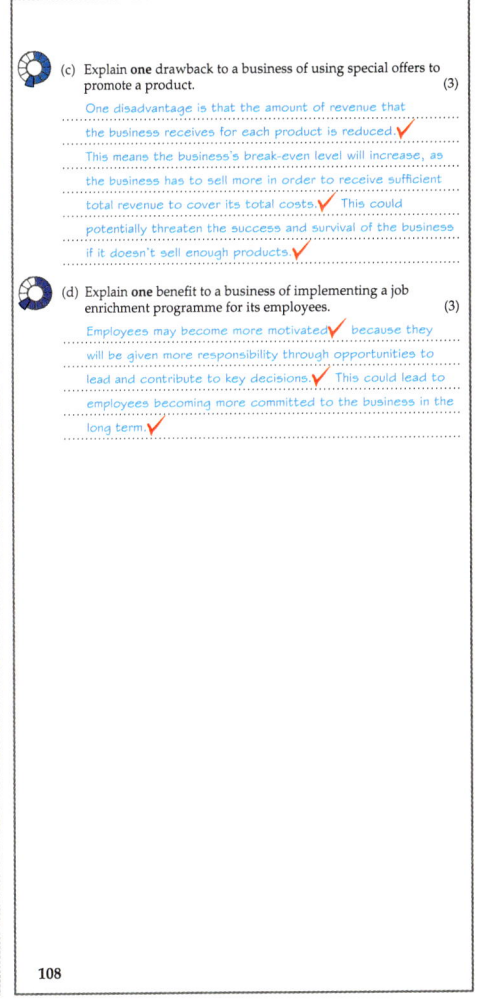

SECTION A
Answer ALL questions. Write your answers in the spaces provided.
Some questions must be answered with a cross in a box ☒.
If you change your mind about an answer, put a line through the box ☒ and then mark your new answer with a cross ☒.

1 (a) Which **one** of the following is an advantage to a business of having a centralised organisational structure?
Select **one** answer. (1)

- ☐ A Decisions are made by people that may know their local customers better
- ☐ B Staff are able to have more input into the decision-making process
- ✓ ☒ C Consistent decisions will be made for the whole organisation
- ☐ D Branch managers may have increased motivation

(b) Which **one** of the following involves allowing potential customers to use a product before purchase?
Select **one** answer. (1)

- ☐ A Advertising
- ☐ B Branding
- ☐ C Special offers
- ✓ ☒ D Product trial

(c) Explain **one** benefit to a business of raising finance by selling assets. (3)

One benefit is that it is a cheaper form of finance compared to loan capital.✓ This is because there is no interest to repay,✓ meaning that fixed costs are lower than they would otherwise be, potentially lowering a business's break-even level of sales.✓

(d) Explain **one** benefit to a business of having a quality control system in place. (3)

One benefit is that no defective products should be released to customers.✓ This is because with quality control, a quality inspector is employed to check that products meet the required standard at the end of the production process.✓ This should lead to a business gaining a good reputation for having quality products/services.✓

(Total for Question 1 = 8 marks)

2 (a) Which **two** of the following are examples of goods?
Select **two** answers. (2)

- ☐ A Hairdressers
- ☐ B Dentists
- ✓ ☒ C Shoes
- ✓ ☒ D Fridge freezer
- ☐ E Travel agent

(b) Which **two** of the following are advantages to a business of internal recruitment?
Select **two** answers. (2)

- ☐ A It is likely to result in a wider range of candidates
- ☐ B There may be a greater variety of fresh ideas
- ☐ C Candidates will always have the skills needed so no training will be required
- ✓ ☒ D It is likely to be quicker and cheaper
- ✓ ☒ E The firm will already be aware of its employees' skills, experiences and attitudes to work

Table 1 contains information about a new piece of equipment that a business will keep and use for four years.

Total profit over four years	£440 000
Cost of equipment	£550 000

Table 1

(c) Using the information in Table 1, calculate the average rate of return of the new equipment. You are advised to show your workings. (2)

Average annual profit = $\frac{440\,000}{4}$ = 110 000

ARR (%) = $\frac{110\,000}{550\,000} \times 100$ = ✓

.... 20 ✓ %

(d) Explain **one** method a business may use to extend the cycle of a product it sells. (3)

Modify the product in some way✓. This is because by modifying the product it makes the product different from the original version✓, therefore loyal customers will be attracted by this and inclined to purchase the upgraded version, extending the product's life.✓

(e) Explain **one** benefit to a business of having a decentralised organisational structure. (3)

One benefit is that the needs of local customers are more likely to be met.✓ This is because the managers of local branches understand their target market better than someone based at head office, so can adapt the product to meet these needs.✓ This could result in sales and revenue increasing for the business.✓

(Total for Question 2 = 12 marks)

3 (a) Which **one** of the following is an example of marketing data that a business could use to help make decisions?
Select **one** answer. (1)

- ✓ ☒ A Customer opinion of a product
- ☐ B Financial accounts of a business
- ☐ C The interest rate that a bank would charge for loan capital
- ☐ D The number of competitors in a market

Figure 1 shows the sales revenue of three businesses that make up the entire market.

[Bar chart showing Sales Revenue (£000s) on y-axis from 0 to 1000. Business A: 600, Business B: 800, Business C: 400]

Figure 1

(b) Using the information in Figure 1, calculate the revenue of Business A as a percentage of the total market revenue. Show your answer to two decimal places. (2)

Total market revenue = 600 000
  800 000
+ 400 000
  1 800 000

% of total market revenue for Business A = $\frac{600\,000}{1\,800\,000} \times 100$ = ✓

.... 33.33 ✓ %

(c) Explain **one** drawback to a business of using special offers to promote a product. (3)

One disadvantage is that the amount of revenue that the business receives for each product is reduced.✓ This means the business's break-even level will increase, as the business has to sell more in order to receive sufficient total revenue to cover its total costs.✓ This could potentially threaten the success and survival of the business if it doesn't sell enough products.✓

(d) Explain **one** benefit to a business of implementing a job enrichment programme for its employees. (3)

Employees may become more motivated✓ because they will be given more responsibility through opportunities to lead and contribute to key decisions.✓ This could lead to employees becoming more committed to the business in the long term.✓

145

Set 3 Paper 2 Answers

(e) Discuss the drawback of insufficient communication to a business. (6)

One drawback is that employees may miss vital information from customers. This could lead to the business not meeting its customers' needs. As a result, the customers may become dissatisfied and therefore may choose to purchase from a rival company in future.

Another drawback is that employees may not know what the business is aiming to achieve and how they can contribute to this, due to a lack of communication from managers. This may lead to them becoming demotivated, which could lead to a large proportion of employees leaving the firm. This would then require the business to recruit new employees, and recruiting new staff is costly.

(Total for Question 3 = 15 marks)
TOTAL FOR SECTION A = 35 MARKS

Writing a good answer

'Discuss' questions ask you to look at a likely impact, benefit, drawback or similar. In a 'Discuss' question you should:
- show your **Knowledge and Understanding (AO1)** by giving one or two clear points
- include a minimum of **five linked development points** across the 1–2 points you have made, to demonstrate your **Analysis (AO3a)**

A very strong answer because…

✓ **Understanding:** Two valid points have been made in two separate paragraphs (employees may miss vital information, and employees may not know what the business is aiming to achieve and how they can contribute).

✓ **Analysis:** There are three linked strands of development in each paragraph, which more than covers the requirement for a minimum of five in total. There is also excellent use of connectives, such as 'therefore' and 'this may lead to', to show these links.

SECTION B
Answer ALL questions
Read the following extract carefully and then answer Questions 4, 5 and 6. Write your answers in the spaces provided.

IKEA is a Swedish-founded multinational retailer that designs and sells ready-to-assemble furniture, kitchen appliances and home accessories. Until now IKEA stores have been huge out-of-town warehouses where customers walk round a large showroom before collecting their furniture from a 'market hall' warehouse at the end. However, this format is changing.

IKEA has recently opened a new city centre shop on Tottenham Court Road, London. The shop is the retailer's revised strategy in the UK to bring IKEA to the heart of urban areas as it tries to respond to the demand from the continued growth of people living in cities. An IKEA spokesperson, IKEA UK and Ireland Country Manager, said that, '*Urbanisation and inner-city living are trends that continue to dominate the market. By launching this new approach and investing in our online offer and services, we are working to ensure IKEA remains affordable, convenient and sustainable, both now and in the future.*'

The new Tottenham Court Road shop will specialise in kitchens and wardrobes, giving customers the advice and inspiration they need to browse, plan and order their furniture. IKEA will offer its customers a bespoke service, using interactive software to help them design their dream rooms at affordable prices.

IKEA has been investing heavily in online, logistics and distribution in a move to cut its home delivery times from one to two weeks to three to four days. An IKEA spokesperson said that this investment was not a reaction to Amazon or any particular retailer but a response to changing customer demands.

IKEA takes pride in how it treats staff members, as it believes that they are the heart of the brand. The retailer invests heavily in its staff, providing many opportunities for job rotation and job enrichment. In 2018, 1,711 workers took a new job opportunity within the business and 523 employees were promoted internally. IKEA hopes that this investment in staff and its new strategy of opening inner-city stores will help the business to continue to grow over the coming years.

(Source adapted from: https://www.ikea.com/gb/en/this-is-ikea/newsroom/press-release/ikea-to-open-new-shop-on-londons-tottenham-court-road-as-part-of-new-city-centre-approach/ and https://www.ikea.com/gb/en/doc/content-snippet-links/ikea-ikea-uk-annual-summary-financial-year-2018__1364661808789.pdf)

---

4 (a) Outline **one** benefit to IKEA of creating a person specification as part of the process of recruiting sales assistants for its new inner-city stores. (2)

It would allow IKEA to alert potential applicants that they will need good communication skills so its staff can talk about kitchen designs with clients. ✓ This will ensure that IKEA gets suitable candidates for the post, who can inspire customers. ✓

The new inner-city IKEA stores will not hold any stock due to the limited amount of space available.

(b) Analyse the impact to IKEA of using just-in-time stock control in its new inner-city stores. (6)

One benefit is that IKEA will not have to hold kitchen appliances or wardrobes on site, therefore rent for this smaller premises will be lower. This is particularly important as the cost of renting retail outlets in inner cities is high, particularly in central London where this first new city centre shop was opened. This will keep the Swedish retailer's costs down, meaning that IKEA can continue to offer furniture at affordable prices, as the IKEA spokesperson stated. This would make IKEA more competitive compared to rivals such as Furniture Village, which may result in customers being more likely to buy from the Swedish retail giant, potentially leading to increased revenues and profits for IKEA.

(Total for Question 4 = 8 marks)

Writing a good answer

In an 'Analyse' question you should:
- clearly **apply** your answer to the **context** throughout (AO2)
- give **one or two clear points** and a minimum of **five linked development points**, to demonstrate your **Analysis (AO3a)**.

A very strong answer because…

✓ **Application:** Context is used throughout the answer, for example 'kitchen appliances', 'an IKEA spokesperson' and 'Furniture Village'.

✓ **Analysis:** The answer describes one valid impact then supports the analysis with more than five linked strands of development.

---

5 Figure 2 shows the total number of yearly website visits on IKEA's site between 2013 and 2018.

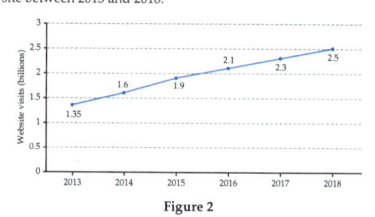

Figure 2 (graph: 2013=1.35, 2014=1.6, 2015=1.9, 2016=2.1, 2017=2.3, 2018=2.5 billions)

Table 2 contains some information regarding IKEA's revenue and net profit in 2017 and 2018.

	2018	2017
Revenue (€ bn)	38.8	38.3
Net profit (€ bn)	1.47	2.47

Table 2

(a) Using the information in Figure 2, calculate, to two decimal places, the percentage increase in IKEA website visits between 2013 and 2018. You are advised to show your workings. (2)

Difference = 2.50 − 1.35 = 1.15 € bn

Percentage increase = Difference / Original value × 100
= 1.15 / 1.35 × 100
= 85.19% ✓

85.19 ✓ %

(b) Using the information in Table 2, calculate, to two decimal places, IKEA's net profit margin in 2018. You are advised to show your workings. (2)

Net profit margin (%) = Net profit / Sales revenue × 100
= 1.47 bn / 38.8 bn × 100 ✓
= 3.79 ✓ %

(c) Analyse the benefit to IKEA of it investing 'heavily in its staff'. (6)

Investing heavily in staff, for example through staff training, will give IKEA's employees better knowledge of the furniture their firm sells. Staff will feel more valued because they are being trained, and are therefore more likely to feel motivated about selling to customers. For example, sales assistants may be more enthusiastic about speaking to customers when they come into the inner-city stores to discuss the bespoke kitchens they want. This will lead to greater customer satisfaction for IKEA's customers, which means they are more likely to purchase from the Swedish retailer and to recommend the company to friends and family.

Another way of investing in staff is promoting them within the company. The case study states that 1711 of IKEA's staff took on new opportunities within the business in 2018, and 523 employees were promoted internally. This means staff will be more likely to commit to the success of the Swedish retail giant. This will benefit IKEA through high staff retention, which means the company will not have to continually recruit more workers for its furniture shops, so helping to keep costs down and leading to IKEA being more competitive than its rivals such as Amazon.

(Total for Question 5 = 10 marks)

Writing a good answer

In an 'Analyse' question you should:
- clearly **apply** your answer to the **context** throughout (AO2)
- give **one or two clear points** and a minimum of **five linked development points**, to demonstrate your **Analysis (AO3a)**.

A very strong answer because…

✓ **Application:** Both paragraphs link back to the case study, for example, 'furniture', 'sales assistants', 'inner-city stores', and 'bespoke kitchens'.

✓ **Analysis:** This answer demonstrates the two-paragraph approach, with more than five linked strands of development overall. There is good use of connectives.

Set 3 Paper 2 Answers

6 (a) State **one** drawback to *IKEA* from selling its products online. (1)
The Swedish furniture retailer will have to compete with a larger number of furniture companies. ✓

(b) Outline **one** benefit to *IKEA* from its use of technology in providing its service in the new inner-city stores. (2)
The Swedish furniture retailer can offer a better customer service ✓ because it can use interactive software to help potential customers design their kitchens. ✓

To continue to see growth in sales, *IKEA* is considering two different options.
Option 1: Continue to invest in large out-of-town stores.
Option 2: Open more inner-city stores that provide a bespoke service.

(c) Justify which **one** of these two options *IKEA* should choose. (9)

I believe that IKEA should focus on Option 2. This is because by offering a bespoke service, such as tailoring the design of a kitchen to the individual customer, IKEA can stand out from home service retailers. This will help the Swedish retailer to add value, meaning that IKEA can sell its furniture for a higher amount without losing lots of customers. This could potentially lead to more profits, which could be reinvested to help finance future inner-city furniture stores.

However, by choosing Option 2, IKEA is moving away from its traditional business model, which has been successful in the past (helping to generate €38.8bn in revenue in 2018). This strategic change may be limiting in terms of the number of customers who are served compared with the huge out-of-town warehouses where customers can self-serve. This model requires workers to spend time with individual customers, potentially limiting the amount of sales of appliances and therefore the company's future growth.

In conclusion, I think that Option 2 is the better option for IKEA – the main reason being that, as the case study states, more and more people are moving to inner-city areas. Therefore, this market is one IKEA needs to appeal to. However, whether IKEA's new stores are successful will ultimately depend on customer preferences and wants. If it becomes clear that the majority of customers prefer the 'market hall' warehouse approach, then Option 1 may ultimately prove more beneficial.

(Total for Question 6 = 12 marks)
TOTAL FOR SECTION B = 30 MARKS

Writing a good answer

'Justify' questions will ask you to make a choice between two options. **There is no need to discuss both options.**

When answering a 'Justify' question, aim to write three paragraphs:
- **Paragraph 1:** Select the option you feel is best and state why, using at least three **linked strands of development** to demonstrate **Analysis (AO3a)**. Make sure you refer to the **context** throughout, to demonstrate **Application (AO2)**.
- **Paragraph 2:** Explain a drawback of the option you have chosen, to show balance and **Evaluation (AO3b)**. Again, include at least three **linked strands of development** to demonstrate **Analysis (AO3a)**, and refer to **context** to demonstrate **Application (AO2)**. By including three linked strands of development in both paragraphs, you can be more confident that you are covering the overall requirement of five linked strands of development for this answer.
- **Paragraph 3:** Conclude by giving the main reason why you selected your option. Use the 'It depends' rule. This is another way of demonstrating **Evaluation (AO3b)**, and should also refer to the context for **Application (AO2)**.

A very strong answer because…

✓ **Application:** The case study is referred to throughout. Clear reference is made to the fact that IKEA will help its customers design their dream kitchen, as well as the revenue figures from Table 2. The answer also identifies the trend for migration to inner cities, as described in the case study.
✓ **Analysis:** The first paragraph contains at least five linked strands of development and there are more linked strands in the second paragraph. There is excellent use of connectives, such as 'therefore', 'this could potentially lead to' and 'this is because', to show these links.
✓ **Evaluation:** The conclusion contains a balanced argument that considers a benefit and a drawback of Option 2. There is a clear statement of the main reason why the student chose Option 2 as well as good consideration of the 'It depends' rule.

SECTION C
Answer ALL questions.
Read the following extract carefully and then answer Question 7.
Write your answers in the spaces provided.

Jack's is a new cut-price brand of supermarket owned by *Tesco* and launched to rival *Aldi* and *Lidl*. The new concept is named after Jack Cohen, who founded *Tesco* 99 years ago. The new venture has been funded through internal finance provided by *Tesco*, with the company investing between £20 and £25 million. *Tesco* CEO, Dave Lewis, indicated that the new model would have a focus on low prices and an emphasis on quality British produce.

This strategy is in response to competition from *Aldi* and *Lidl*, who have increased their market share to 13.1 per cent over the past five years. The supermarket industry is changing and, as *Aldi's* and *Lidl's* success proves, customers are turning to cheaper shops.

Lewis hopes to open 15 more *Jack's* stores across the country within a year and to employ 250 new employees. The staff will be recruited externally and will earn a 'base rate' of £9 per hour, which is 58p more than a *Tesco* worker (as at November 2018). However, *Jack's* workers won't get a 10 per cent discount as *Tesco* staff do, and they will not enjoy any bonuses. As part of a strategy of keeping costs down, staff will be able to wear their own clothes, with only an apron and a name badge necessary.

Jack's will stock around 2 600 products of which 1 800 will be own-label items (a typical *Tesco* stocks more than 25 000 items). It will stock some household brands such as *Coca-Cola* but the focus is on *Jack's* own-label products.

Lewis stated that *Jack's* will use the company's existing supply base to keep costs down and that this, combined with more efficient, cheaper-to-run stores, will mean customers get a better deal.

(Source: https://inews.co.uk/news/consumer/everything-you-need-to-know-about-jacks-tesco/)

---

7 (a) Define the term external recruitment. (1)
Appointing a new employee from outside the existing staff. ✓

Figure 3 shows the market share (of the total grocery market) of *Tesco*, *Aldi* and *Lidl* between 2014 and 2018.

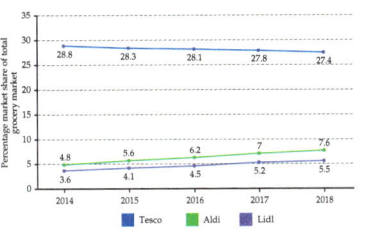

Figure 3
(Source: https://www.statista.com/statistics/300656/grocery-market-share-in-great-britain-year-on-year-comparison/)

(b) Using Figure 3, identify which of the supermarkets saw a decrease in its market share between 2014 and 2018. (1)
Tesco ✓

Table 3 shows some financial information relating to *Tesco* for 2017 and 2018.

	2017 (£ million)	2018 (£ million)
Revenue	55 917	57 491
Cost of sales	53 015	54 141
Other operating expenses	1 995	1 663

Table 3
(Source://www.tescoplc.com/media/474793/tesco_ar_2018.pdf)

(c) Using Table 3, calculate *Tesco's* gross profit for 2018. You are advised to show your workings. (2)

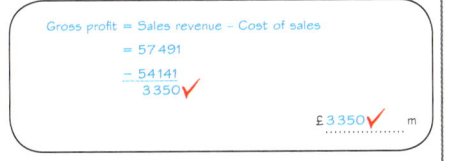

Gross profit = Sales revenue − Cost of sales
= 57 491
− 54 141
3 350 ✓

£ 3 350 ✓ m

147

Set 3 Paper 2 Answers

To improve the productivity of staff and therefore the performance of the business, Jack's is considering two different methods of motivation.

Option 1: Increase the annual salary of workers.
Option 2: Pay workers a bonus based on the success of the store.

(d) Justify which **one** of these two options Jack's should choose. (9)

I believe that Jack's should choose Option 2, because if the supermarket's staff know they will get paid more money if they sell more groceries, they will work hard to ensure that sales levels are high. This could potentially help Jack's to become competitive against rival supermarket chains such as Aldi and Lidl, allowing it to increase its market share in the grocery market as customers start to switch supermarket brands.

However, paying staff, such as checkout staff, a bonus could have very little impact on motivation if it is paid due to the amount of sales made. This is because the workers in a supermarket are not trying to encourage shoppers to buy more food, therefore they may feel that their performance has very little impact on whether the supermarket makes money or not. They may feel that they can work extremely hard and it wouldn't impact on whether customers bought more food or not, therefore the offer of a bonus may not make the checkout operators more productive.

In conclusion, I think Option 2 is the best option. The most significant reason as to why is that the supermarket is operating in a market where low prices are demanded by consumers and although paying bonuses increases costs, they would only be paid if the business was successful, meaning that the business could afford to pay it without having to increase prices. Also, over the short-term, the discount supermarket staff would be receiving a higher salary than an equivalent worker in a Tesco store, so the level of their salary would be considered fair in relation to other supermarket employers. However, it will depend on how the award of the bonus is assessed – if it is just purely linked to food sales it won't work, as their performance doesn't impact on the amount shoppers buy, but if it can be linked to an employee's targets then it could make Jack's staff more productive.

Writing a good answer

'Justify' questions will ask you to make a choice between two options. **There is no need to discuss both options.**

When answering a 'Justify' question, aim to write three paragraphs:
- **Paragraph 1:** Select the option you feel is best and state why, using at least three linked strands of development to demonstrate **Analysis (AO3a)**. Make sure you refer to the context throughout, to demonstrate **Application (AO2)**.
- **Paragraph 2:** Explain a drawback of the option you have chosen, to show balance and **Evaluation (AO3b)**. Again, include at least three linked strands of development to demonstrate **Analysis (AO3a)**, and refer to context to demonstrate **Application (AO2)**.
By including three linked strands of development in both paragraphs, you can be more confident that you are covering the overall requirement of five linked strands of development for this answer.
- **Paragraph 3:** Conclude by giving the main reason why you selected your option. Use the 'It depends' rule. This is another way of demonstrating **Evaluation (AO3b)**, and should also refer to the context for **Application (AO2)**.

A very strong answer because...

✓ **Application:** In all three paragraphs, repeated references are made to the discount grocery market, including in the conclusion where the main reason for the choice is clearly linked to Jack's situation.
✓ **Analysis:** The first two paragraphs each contain three linked strands of development, meaning there are more than the five linked strands of development. The answer makes excellent use of connectives, such as 'this is because', 'therefore' and 'this could potentially', to show these links.
✓ **Evaluation:** There is a balanced consideration of why paying Jack's employees a bonus may or may not be motivating. There is also a detailed conclusion that clearly justifies what the most significant reason is and considers what it might depend on.

(e) Evaluate whether having lower prices than competitors is the best way for Jack's to compete in the grocery market. You should use the information provided as well as your knowledge of business. (12)

Having low prices is essential for Jack's to be competitive. Jack's main rivals are Aldi and Lidl, who are well-known for their ability to sell groceries at prices well below the major supermarkets. This means that to meet the needs of potential customers, prices need to be low. As the majority of the products Jack's are proposing to sell are the store's own-branded goods, this is something that is achievable for the grocery store, which will help to attract customers from its discount rivals, potentially leading to the newly-formed supermarket establishing itself in the market.

Having lower prices isn't the only way to compete. As Dave Lewis mentions, the discount supermarket could focus on quality British produce. As consumers are now very conscious as to where their food comes from, promoting the fact that products are British and homegrown will appeal to a sizeable number of customers. This may attract customers away from Aldi and Lidl, who may not promote local produce as much. This could lead to the discount store making more revenue and potentially profit, which could be reinvested back into this venture by the directors of Tesco to grow its market share further.

In conclusion, I believe that having lower prices than competitors is the best way to compete because ultimately it is what the market is saying it wants. Figure 3 shows that market share for discount stores is growing and Tesco needs to adopt a similar tactic to compete with them. However, it depends what Jack's rivals are doing. Jack's may be just one of the discount stores who may all have similar pricing structures. If this is the case then perhaps it needs some other form of differentiation to go alongside the low prices in order to be the discount supermarket of choice, such as using and promoting British-grown produce.

(Total for Question 7 = 25 marks)
TOTAL FOR SECTION C = 25 MARKS
TOTAL FOR PAPER = 90 MARKS

Writing a good answer

In an 'Evaluate' question you should aim for three paragraphs.
- **Paragraph 1:** Show your **Knowledge and Understanding (AO1)**; for example, give a definition of one of the key terms. You should also use Business terms throughout. Then provide an argument in support of the statement, with at least three linked development points to show thorough **Analysis (AO3a)**. Apply your points to the context throughout (AO2).
- **Paragraph 2:** Give alternative arguments, with at least three linked development points to show thorough **Analysis (AO3a)**. Apply your points to the context throughout (AO2).
By including three linked strands of development in both paragraphs, you can be more confident that you are covering the overall requirement of five linked strands of development for this answer.
- **Paragraph 3:** Give a balanced conclusion to demonstrate your **Evaluation (AO3b)**, making use of the 'It depends' argument.

A very strong answer because...

✓ **Understanding:** Good business terminology and theory have been used throughout. The response demonstrates a sound understanding of why having low prices will help Jack's compete in the grocery market and that quality is a method of competing.
✓ **Application:** The response is rooted in the context of the discount grocery market. Excellent reference is made to the case study, for example to highlight that Jack's could compete on the quality of its British produce. The conclusion refers to the case study as well as data in Figure 3.
✓ **Analysis:** There are more than the five linked strands of development across the points made in the first two paragraphs. There is excellent use of connectives, such as 'which will help to', 'this may attract' and 'this could lead to', to show these links.
✓ **Evaluation:** There is a balanced argument in response to the question – setting out the case for why low prices are essential (it is what customers want) while also considering the necessity of quality. There is also effective use of the 'It depends' rule, pointing out how Jack's decision may depend on the need to differentiate itself from its rivals within the discount grocery market.

Published by Pearson Education Limited, 80 Strand, London, WC2R 0RL.

www.pearsonschoolsandfecolleges.co.uk

Copies of official specifications for all Pearson qualifications may be found on the website: qualifications.pearson.com

Text and illustrations © Pearson Education Ltd 2020
Typeset and illustrated by Newgen KnowledgeWorks Pvt. Ltd., Chennai, India
Editorial and project management services by Newgen Publishing UK
Cover illustration by Miriam Sturdee

The right of Paul Clark and Andrew Redfern to be identified as authors of this work has been asserted by them in accordance with the Copyright, Designs and Patents Act 1988.

First published 2020

23 22 21 20
10 9 8 7 6 5 4 3 2 1

British Library Cataloguing in Publication Data
A catalogue record for this book is available from the British Library

ISBN 978 1 292 29676 0

Copyright notice
All rights reserved. No part of this publication may be reproduced in any form or by any means (including photocopying or storing it in any medium by electronic means and whether or not transiently or incidentally to some other use of this publication) without the written permission of the copyright owner, except in accordance with the provisions of the Copyright, Designs and Patents Act 1988 or under the terms of a licence issued by the Copyright Licensing Agency, 5th Floor, Shackleton House, Hay's Galleria, 4 Battle Bridge Lane, London SE1 2HX (www.cla.co.uk). Applications for the copyright owner's written permission should be addressed to the publisher.

Printed in Italy by L.E.G.O. S.p.A.

Acknowledgements
The author and publisher would like to thank the following individuals and organisations for their kind permission to reproduce copyright material.

Image Credit(s):
Alamy Stock Photo: Geoffrey Robinson 118, 147, **Getty Images Incorporated:** Archideaphoto/iStock 15,127, BankLT/iStock Editorial 28, 127, Silvy_/iStock 36,127, ThreeDiCube/iStock 49,131, Thinkstock Images/Stockbyte 90,142, **Just Eat:** 28,130, **Shutterstock:** Oleksandr Rozdobudko 8,126, Wozzie 28,76,127,139, TY Lim 36,131, Ziggysofi 56,134, SpeedKingz 97, 143, Photobyphm 110,146, **Travelodge** 69, 138.

Text Credits:
P 28, 130: Subway trials delivery with Just Eat, June 2018, © Subway IP LLC. Used with permission; **P 71, 138:** Report and Financial Statements, For the year ended 31 December 2018, © 2018, Thame and London Limited; **P 77, 139:** Graph sourced from M&S to lose its decades long status as the number one clothing retailer to Primark, May 22, 2018, © GlobalData Plc 2019. Retrieved from https://www.globaldata.com/ms-lose-decades-long-status-number-one-clothing-retailer-primark/. Used with permission; **P 110, 146:** IKEA to open new shop on London's Tottenham Court Road as part of new city centre approach by IKEA, 23rd July 2018, IKEA/Javier Quinones. © Inter IKEA Systems B.V. Used with permission; **P 112, 146:** Data adapted from: IKEA Facts and Figures 2013-2018, IKEA FINANCIAL YEAR Report, retrieved from https://highlights.ikea.com/2018/facts-and-figures/home/, © Inter IKEA Systems B.V.; **P 119, 147:** Adapted from Market share of grocery stores in Great Britain from August 2012 to August 2018. © Statista 2019. Retrieved from https://www.statista.com/statistics/300656/grocery-market-share-in-great-britain-year-on-year-comparison/.

All other images © Pearson Education

Notes from the publisher
1. While the publishers have made every attempt to ensure that advice on the qualification and its assessment is accurate, the official specification and associated assessment guidance materials are the only authoritative source of information and should always be referred to for definitive guidance.
   Pearson examiners have not contributed to any sections in this resource relevant to examination papers for which they have responsibility.
2. Pearson has robust editorial processes, including answer and fact checks, to ensure the accuracy of the content in this publication, and every effort is made to ensure this publication is free of errors. We are, however, only human, and occasionally errors do occur. Pearson is not liable for any misunderstandings that arise as a result of errors in this publication, but it is our priority to ensure that the content is accurate. If you spot an error, please do contact us at resourcescorrections@pearson.com so we can make sure it is corrected.

Answers

For your own notes